AF342587

Four in Glass

Carl Hasse

Masami Koda

Asa Sandlund

Preston Singletary

Matthew Kangas

Guest Curator

FOVA
Texas Tech University
Lubbock
1997

Essay © 1997 by **Matthew Kangas**

All rights reserved

ISBN 0-9650808-2-X

Printed and bound in the United States of America by Printech, Lubbock, Texas.

Distributed by

FOVA Galleries

Department of Art

Box 42081

Texas Tech University

Lubbock, Texas 79409-2081.

tel: (806) 742-1947; FAX (806) 742-1971.

Photography

Richard Nicol (Carl Hasse and Masami Koda)

Roger Schreiber (Asa Sandlund and Preston Singletary, including portraits)

Douglas Tucker (portraits of Carl Hasse and Masami Koda)

Russell Johnson and Geoff Lee (studio shots of Asa Sandlund and Preston Singletary)

Design

Prashant Agarwal, Steven Henderson

Front Cover

Preston Singletary, *Prestonuzzi Pair* (detail), 1996-97

Blown glass, 23 by 12 in. diam.; 8 by 12 in. diam.

Courtesy of William Traver Gallery, Seattle

Preface

Four in Glass is a major glass exhibition that makes October, 1997 a significant month for FOVA Galleries of the Texas Tech University Department of Art. Work by emerging artists in the field of glass artistry provides our students, community, and surrounding region an opportunity to interpret and interact with works of national and international excellence.

Providing the highest opportunities in the visual arts for our audience requires many people and organizations coming together with the same vision. FOVA would like to express its gratitude to those whose support helped this vision become a reality. We extend our appreciation to CH Foundation and The Helen Jones Foundation for their continued financial support. We would like to extend recognition and thanks to Matthew Kangas, guest curator of the exhibition and author of the catalog essay; Prashant Agarwal, designer of the catalog; Bill Bagley, whose idea initiated this exhibition; and to the gallery staff, Marjorie Arnett and Julie Zager.

Most of all, FOVA offers its deepest appreciation to the four artists whose work is represented in this catalog: Carl Hasse, Masami Koda, Asa Sandlund, and Preston Singletary. For help in the coordination and shipping of the objects by Preston Singletary, I also wish to thank William Traver and Megan Woo of the William Traver Gallery, Seattle, Washington; and for help with Masami Koda's and Asa Sandlund's work, Julie Woo of Vetri International Glass, Seattle, also deserves thanks. The superb photography was done by Roger Schreiber and Richard Nicol.

Shawn F. Holz
Interim Director

Four in Glass *Carl Hasse* By Matthew Kangas
Masami Koda
Asa Sandlund
Preston Singletary

American studio glass is now pushing into its third generation of artists. The four young artists in this exhibition exemplify the best and most diverse of that generation, one that has chosen glass to convey its ideas used in isolation, or in combination with other materials.

Since the two experimental workshops at Toledo Museum of Art in 1962, when Harvey K. Littleton and Dominick Labino came up with a small portable furnace and a batch formula for melting glass at a lower temperature, "studio glass" has become the operative term. Such a development liberated artists from the factory setting, freeing them up to explore ideas instead of only production, and allowing them to work at home or in a studio situation. They could then better encounter the many qualities of glass that so appeal to viewers: transparency, fragility, color, malleability, liquidity, and solidity.

The artists in *Four in Glass*—Carl Hasse, Masami Koda, Asa Sandlund, and Preston Singletary—choose highly varied technical approaches to the medium and, in so doing, offer us beautiful and often surprising results. For Hasse, the youngest, glass is a supplementary medium to reinforce his investigation of American consumerism, subcultures, and medieval or Renaissance medical and botanical illustrations. For Japanese-born Koda, glass embodies nature in its infinite variety: growth, decay, ecology, air, and fire. With Sandlund, graphic design is explored in glass as a semiotic world wherein we are con-

stantly surrounded by signs, typefaces and industrial containers. Singletary became a glass artist through the time-honored Italian tradition of apprenticeship and mastery transplanted to Seattle. His mature treatment of Italian glassblowing techniques dating back to the tenth century A.D. is reinvigorating the field with his revival of 1960s Scandinavian design shapes. Looking far back in time, as well as back a few decades, Singletary confounds our expectations of what glass vases are because he renders them largely unusable at the same time he attenuates their forms.

After Littleton's and Labino's breakthroughs, another artist became a pioneer in the revival of American glass art outside the factory setting, Dale Chihuly. Awarded a Fulbright grant to study in Italy at the Venini factory on Murano Island in 1966, Chihuly was restricted by the company from actually blowing any glass but was allowed to observe the crews day after day. Little did the Venetians know that by even allowing him to watch, some of their tightly held secrets (since 970 A.D., the birth of European glassblowing in Venice) would flee to the New World and, not only create American studio glass but, in the long run, rehabilitate Muranese glass through the many cultural exchanges with artists and technicians Chihuly subsequently brought about. His co-founding in 1971 of the Pilchuck Glass School with John Hauberg and Anne Gould Hauberg made possible guest workshops that occurred over the ensuing 26 years and brought together artists, students, and interested amateurs from all over the world.

All the artists in *Four in Glass* have ties to the Pilchuck Glass School. They either worked, studied or taught there. Hasse, for example, was an outstanding Emerging Artist in Residence in 1993, who then chose to remain in the Seattle area to work and make art, partly because of the cheap rent and availability of studio space, partly because of his attraction to the underground punk scene and the proximity of natural beauty. He subsequently held jobs at Chihuly, Inc., the artist's vast studio and showroom setting on the north shore of Seattle's Lake Union.

Koda continues to work periodically for another major glass artist, Ginny Ruffner, an internationally hailed artist who virtually singlehandedly revived and created art-world respect for the benighted lampworking technique. She is known particularly for her encouragement of younger artists.

Singletary has worked for Benjamin Moore, a Rhode Island School of Design-trained artist and designer, who is a crucial link to the visiting Italians for whom Singletary has crewed on the hot shop floor and who have, in turn, influenced the elegance of the younger artist's glass. While in Sweden giving a workshop at the Kosta Boda factory, he met a young Swedish graphic designer, Asa Sandlund. They married and returned to Seattle where Sandlund continued her own interest in glass as a vehicle for homages to typography and for her own additions to the Swedish tradition of modern glass art.

Taken together, these four young artists reflect the extraordinary diversity of approaches to contemporary studio glass. In addition to the traditional appeals of glass—color, transparency, delicacy—they add subject matters of arcane science; ecology, typography; and postwar design-style revivals. With Hasse and Koda on the fringe of the establishment craft art world, and Sandlund and Singletary more plugged in to the mainstream, all four artists are part of an encouraging phenomenon that has pushed studio glass into the forefront of American craft materials today. Twenty years ago, ceramics ruled the day in terms of respect, originality and art-world acceptance. Today, these roles have been adopted by artists using glass. The four under discussion here are sure to have an impact in the coming years.

Carl Hasse

Youngest of the artists on view, Carl Hasse seems at first to be the farthest away from traditional technical approaches to glass, not to mention from straightforward imagery of ornament or decoration. However, upon closer inspection, it becomes clear that, while Hasse is presenting a virtual non-technique or anti-craft appearance, his powers of construction and execution are still unthinkable without substantial training and experience.

Rejecting blowing, Hasse opts for painting in fired-on enamels on sheets of clear stained-glass-quality glass or even on recycled automotive glass initially sandblasted before painting.

Hasse's recent work since graduating from Alfred University in 1993 explores two distinct themes: transformations of found automotive repair catalog ads or illustrations; and reconfigurations of historical representations of botanical specimens associated with alchemical or occult practices. At the same time, he has a fascination with obsolete tools such as medieval childbirthing forceps in *Braun's Craniolast* (1994). As is often the case in his art, the imagery initially seems unclear, unrecognizable or illegible. When we look more closely, however, or examine it in the light of his purported investigations, images emerge as if under a microscope. The blurring or crowding of images in his work proposes an image-saturated world but not one mediated through photography. Instead, there is a sense of primal discovery or encounter, like a child's focussing in on a complicated sight for the first time.

Metro Lift (1993), *Bachelor Pad* and *Chevelle* (both 1994) examine the anatomy of the American male's obsession with cars. With the cutaway aerial floorplan in *Bachelor Pad*, Hasse equates the guy's van with a home worthy of vagabonds—or even disgruntled postal employees. *Car* (1995) and *Chevelle* isolate the schematic vehicle on green-tinted and sandblasted glass backgrounds that also resemble recycled auto glass. Rendered thus as central icons, they are affectionate targets of reverence.

With the altered botanical specimens and ancient tools, Hasse is subtly directing us to recall how quickly technology dates itself despite claims for instantaneousness and bravura breakthroughs. About *Braun's*

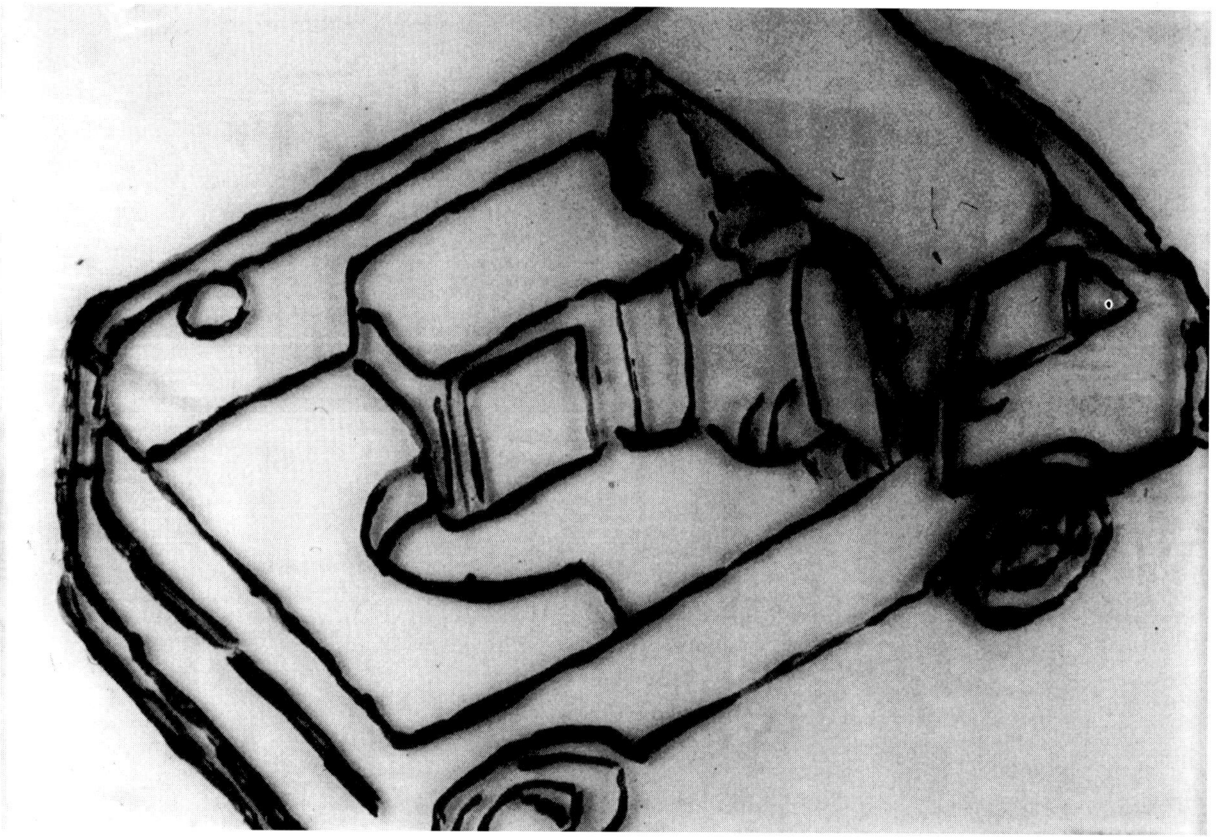

Carl Hasse: **Bachelor Pad**, 1994, Fired-on enamel on glass, 8 by 11 in., Courtesy of the artist.

Craniolast, a vertical diptych depicting forceps and a "birthing hook," Hasse has said

> I paint primitive birthing tools to symbolize the concept (of having to radically change one's lifestyle in order to survive). These tools help extract the baby from its mother, i.e., jump from one world to another. These particular tools are used in a stillborn situation; in all aspects of change, there is some risk involved and childbirth is not exempt. (interview with author, April 1, 1997)

With *Toolshed* (1996), the bulging and elongated forms in the upper panel resemble wooden mallets but they may also be seen as possibly outlines of mushrooms. Dark brown against light brown, the accumulation or pile suggests both organic and manmade "tools." Hasse has explored the mushroom dichotomy (tasty/dangerous) elsewhere in shelf-mounted pieces like *Carousel Center* (1994) and *Time Span: Zero* (1995).

Peyote Buds and *Mandrake People* (1997) is an ambitious four-part work harkening back to floral decoration of glass (see Bohemian crystal) but updating the older convention by the restricted black-and-white palette and its allusions to medieval and Renaissance enthusiasms for the purported curative (and aphrodisiacal) properties of the mandrake root. Juxtaposed with the "mandrake people" are mock-scientific close-ups of peyote cactus buds which are part of Native American spiritual practice. Hasse is uniting the Old World with the New World, reminding us that indigenous spiritual practices were contemporaneous with alchemy and European magic. The four rectangular sections stacked two-on-two resemble parchment-paper pages, spoofing the preciousness of medieval manuscripts. With the sandblasting and enameling, opacity rather than transparency is stressed, further underlining an anti-craft aesthetic pervasive throughout Hasse's work. By alluding to spiritual and medical procedures centuries old the 26-year-old artist is addressing contemporary relationships to Nature in this technological age, our self-destructive attitude as a society, and how they relate to our own mortality (Ibid.).

Ourobouros (1997) concludes the series on view with a depiction of the ancient Greek myth of the snake devouring its own tail. Recurrent in medieval alchemy, the myth suggests the cyclical nature of life. With his combination of glass and painted tin, Hasse accentuates an *arte-povera* or "poor materials" stance vis-à-vis the shiny luxe of studio glass. He risks accusations of the tacky, cheesy or sloppy but redeems himself through the compilation of richly allusive imagery, refreshing informality of construction, and a sense of an ongoing project of artistic discovery and open-ended investigation.

Masami Koda

Masami Koda is exploring the relationship between humanity and nature. She sets for herself a powerful material dichotomy or possible contradiction by using the forthright beauty of glass to embody the destructive power of nature. Although living in the U.S. since 1989, Koda has kept up ties to her parents and family in Kobe, Japan. Like Carl Hasse, Masami Koda is a graduate of Alfred

University, site of the New York State College of Ceramics, the nation's oldest accredited clay program and a magnet for talented art students with an interest in craft materials like clay and glass.

Life and death are the two continuing themes in the art of Masami Koda, the hopefulness present in the "life force" of nature, and the desolation and destructive side of nature as seen in disasters like the 1995 Kobe earthquake. Two works, *Departure* and *200/1 (1-17-95)* (both 1995), deal with the life-and-death aspects of the cataclysmic event. Echoing the "ourobouros" circle shape in Carl Hasse's work, *Departure* is a ring of small copper-oxide-stained bottles, each containing a feather, each capped with white pieces of paper. To Koda's strongly symbolic imagination, the feathers represent

> "the souls of the victims [of the Kobe earthquake], their individual humanity". —(interview with the author, March 31, 1997)

Seen close-up, each smoky smudge also reveals a fingerprint, frequently the only identifying quality for the temblor's victims. But the circular, wheel-like shape also suggests an endless reiteration of movement, and the "captive souls" symbolized by the feathers suggest awaiting release or redemption. The viewer is left with an elegiac feeling, a frustration with the terminality of catastrophe.

By contrast, *200/1 (1-17-95)* is much more complex and satisfying in both its accumulation of symbolic elements and in its more hopeful resolution of disaster. With one in two hundred injured or killed by the earthquake, Koda's title honors them along with the fateful date, January 17, 1995. This time, the victims are represented by elongated stems with floral blooms at each tip. Underneath this morass, small houses represent the damaged manmade world. The entire sculpture emerges out of a lotus-flower base, the traditional Buddhist image of purity and transformation of the soul. Unlike *Departure, 200/1 (1-17-95)* has outward motion like blooms yearning for the sun and its life-sustaining powers.

The positive, life-giving quality inherent in the sun is paid direct homage in *Sunflower* (1997), a more distilled companion to *200/1 (1-17-95)*. Spherical in its overall construct, *Sunflower* lampworked glass in an extraordinary tour-de-force requiring many hours of studio time along with meticulous powers of assembly.

Its transparent green petals seemingly ruffling in the wind, *Sunflower* is not meant to be a literal sunflower or botanical specimen (à la Paul Stankard, a maker of botanical rarities encased in glass) but a generalized flower as "life force." The fiery red upper petals surround small yellow and golden pods or buds at the sculpture's center. The explosive exuberance of the sculpture is further reinforced by the sense of *unopened* buds, as if even more energy were about to be released. Hypnotic and dazzling, *Sunflower* is also weirdly threatening. Both organic and lifeless, its glassy qualities remind us of the artificiality of art, its limited powers of exuding "life force" due to brittle characteristics. Like Hasse, Koda is caught depicting nature in an obviously fakey medium, glass.

As in the other sculptures, in *Sunflower*, too, Koda addresses life and death, in this case, life and the unavoidable fakey quality of nature that is still an ever-present part of contemporary life. As she has commented, it was only once she arrived in the Pacific Northwest especially that she was able to experience nature in an unbounded way, completely unlike the restrictive experience of nature in modern-day Japan (Ibid.). That said, if we willingly enter into Koda's own view of nature, then we can fully appreciate her growing achievements—and promise.

The repeated element is another uniting aspect of Masami Koda's art. *Departure* has its bottles; *200/2 (1-17-95)* has its petals and leaves; *Sunflower* has its blossoms and hidden buds. All these works were foreshadowed as examples of repetitive elements by an important installation piece, *Junin Toiro* (1993), that the artist assembled while still in graduate school at Alfred. Loosely translated as "many men, many minds," *Junin Toiro* consists of cast-glass ears, each set in a pile of sand on the floor. The disembodied ears, alert yet isolated, remain one of Koda's most haunting images.

Similarly, on a much more reduced scale, *Harmony Bowl* (1993) fuses clear-glass hands to form an open-work container shape. Community is the operative reference in *Harmony Bowl*, perfectly expressed by the outstretched, connected hands.

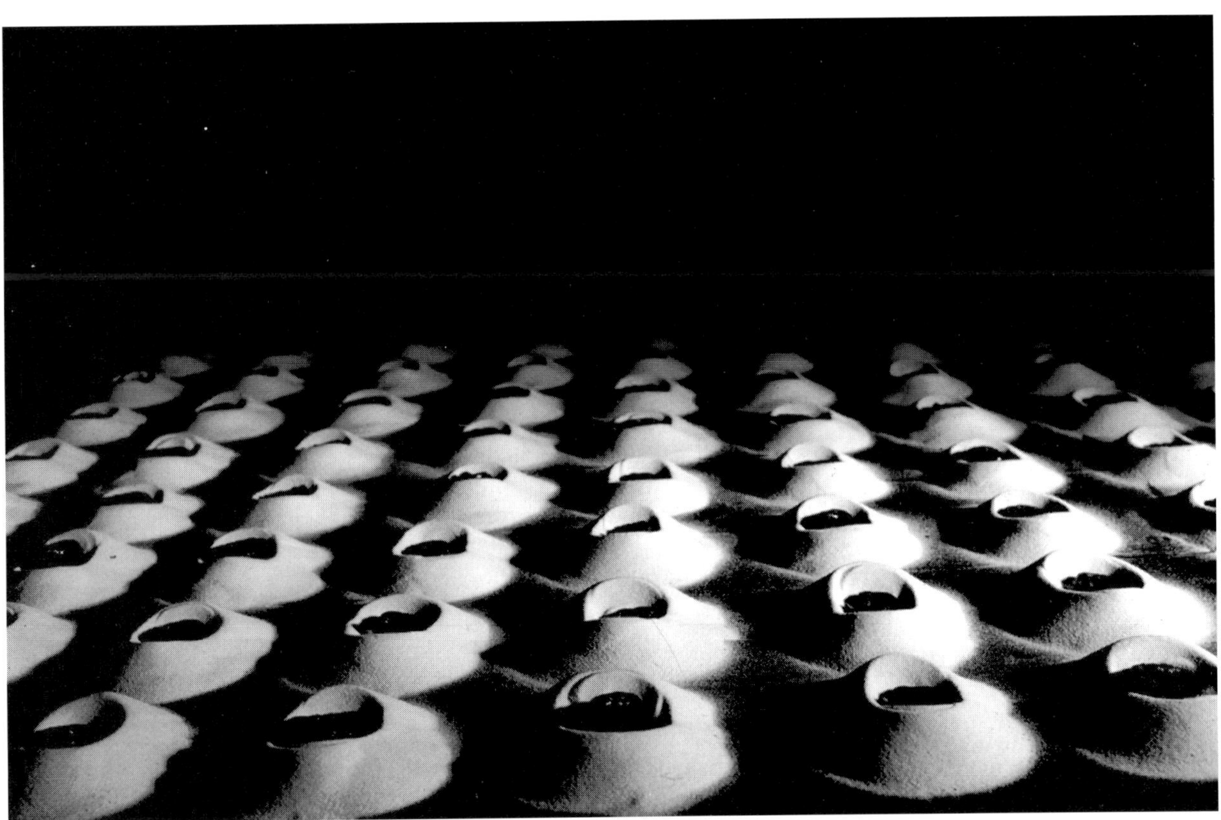

Masami Koda: **Junin Toiro**, 1993 (detail), Cast glass and sand, 10 by 100 ft., Courtesy of the artist.

Taking the idea of the repetitive module and combining it with images of natural growth or cell division, *Life Force* (1997) balances her tendency to use repeated elements with an asymmetrical composition. After the horrors of the Kobe earthquake, life now begins at an elemental, basic level, all the more precious after the huge scale of natural disasters. All the parts are the same sanded or etched clear glass but, as in real life, each "cell" is a completely different size and irregular shape. Assembled like a pearl necklace (or DNA strand), *Life Force* is a quietly powerful work, continuing Koda's pursuit of natural imagery but shoving it forward with more ambiguous imagery and greater autonomous sculptural presence.

A companion piece, *Untitled* (1997), is also wall-mounted yet counters the rounded forms of *Life Force* with spiky connected leaf or bud shapes that meet in overlapping arcs. Pushing the limit of suggesting nature, *Untitled* (1997) asserts its sculptural quality most acutely of all. Now highly generalized, Koda's allusions to nature are no longer necessary to perceive in order to appreciate the sculpture's overall impact. Still, I have a feeling nature will always remain a starting point for her. After all, as we have seen, it contains both life and death.

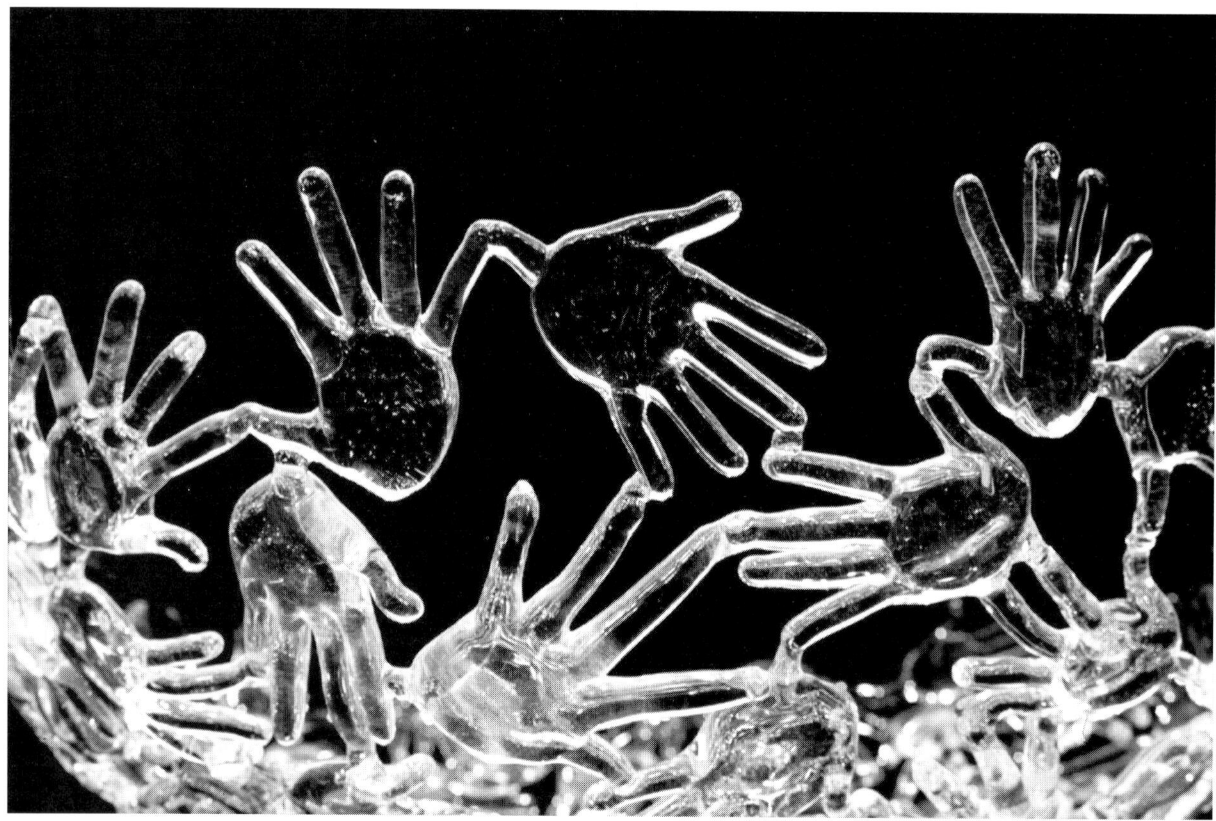

Masami Koda: **Harmony Bowl**, 1993 (detail), Lampworked glass, Courtesy of the artist.

Asa Sandlund

While Hasse and Koda are acting in the American tradition of the artist-designer also being the maker, Asa Sandlund represents the European tradition of the artist being only the designer and someone else being the maker. This is a perfectly honorable approach with many illustrious predecessors including Josiah Wedgwood and Alvar Aalto. What distinguishes Sandlund from her historical forerunners is that her designs for glass are *about design*, specifically, the history of typography. Postmodern in the sense of appropriating other artists' ideas, as well as expressing a self-consciousness about art history, Sandlund pushes art toward text yet never arrives at text art per se. Instead, she is cultivating the handmade nature of lettering and reminding us how letters began as hand-carved or individually drawn alphabets.

Her extensive educational background in Sweden, France, Great Britain and the U.S. exposed Sandlund to a wide range of graphic design approaches. In her glass, Sandlund meditates on the origins of famous typefaces of the twentieth century. These seem so familiar and recognizable to anyone who reads yet her isolation of them onto blown and sand-blasted plates magnifies their individual character. Single letters, not words, become the image-focus for each work and, in lieu of any referential or linguistic meaning, the viewer is forced to contemplate the letters for their own sake, for art's sake.

The lower-case "g" in *Bodoni* (1996) is surely one of the most familiar and innovative of alphabet letters designed in this century with its curving connecting lines between upper and lower circular shapes. With the glass colored and then sandblasted through cut-out stencils, *Bodoni* elevates both the letter "g" and the Bodoni typeface to iconic status.

Rockwell (1996) varies typeface size of the letter "y." Capped by horizontal lines or "serifs," the letter "y" in Rockwell typeface has a formal, finished look that is countered by the rocking motion of the positioned letters across the plate's surface.

Because of Sandlund's recognition within Sweden as a promising young graphic artist and glass designer, she bears the considerable weight of the Scandinavian design tradition, probably most influential in the two decades after World War II. If Swedish design is to regain its primacy of influence in Europe and the U.S., it may be because of talented young artists like Asa Sandlund.

By surveying typography history, Sandlund reminds us that graphic design was among the first of the applied arts to have a global impact. In works like *Frutiger* (1996), she honors those contributions by transforming the upper-case letter "K" into a patterning element by pairing and reversing the letter, underscoring it, and precisely positioning the resulting pattern across a red background.

Other works like *Courier* (1996) (a classic IBM typewriter typeface), *Helvetica* (1996) (the classic sans-serif Swiss typeface), and *Fraktur* (1996) refer to a history that ranges back several centuries, however refined they became in this one. *Fraktur* echoes German Gothic movable type of the Gutenberg era. Indeed, Sandlund's entire typography-on-glass project also may be seen as an updating of the

European tradition of illuminated manuscripts with initial capital letters of important
texts often highly ornamented. For
Sandlund's purposes, the letter itself becomes
the focus of reverence, moving it away from
the printing press or computer, back to the
realm of the handmade.

The *Dimensions* series is closer in origin
to postwar modern Scandinavian design.
However, unlike Preston Singletary, Sandlund
violates the perfect form of the graceful
Swedish vases of the 1950s and 1960s by hav-
ing the *Dimensions* vases cut and faceted on
the top and sides. With color overlays that are
then cut into to reveal clear sections, the
Dimensions are x-ray versions of vases. As we
see through them, we are reminded of the
inner empty space. Although the sides are
gently bulging curves, Sandlund clips the top
off to match the bottom. With the vase mouth

so bluntly terminated (and then smoothed
and polished), each work takes on a contemporary look that is at odds with the well-man-
nered look of most Swedish vases.

Another crucial difference to bear in
mind is that Sandlund's *Dimensions* are all
handmade, not at all dedicated to the mass
production so dear to the Swedish export
industry. In this sense, she is part of a broader
movement in Scandinavian crafts that rejects
the machine-made in favor of work that is
more ambiguous. The *Dimensions* are tooled, to
be sure, elaborately and painstakingly so, but
they still have a cold, abrupt look that teases us
into imagining the presence of something
more mechanical than a live hot shop crew.

Sandlund is exploring "how we perceive shape" in the vases with see-through
holes. Not strictly illusionistic, they nonethe-

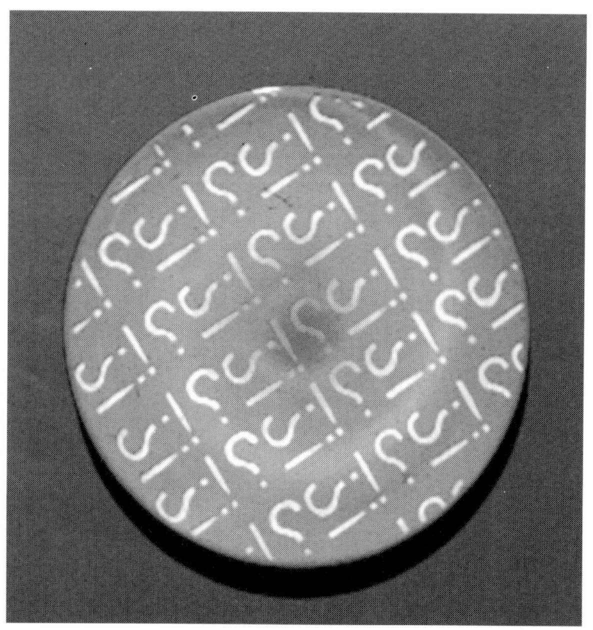

Asa Sandlund: **Helvetica**, 1996
Blown and sandblasted glass, 1 by 18 in. diam.
Courtesy of Vetri International Glass

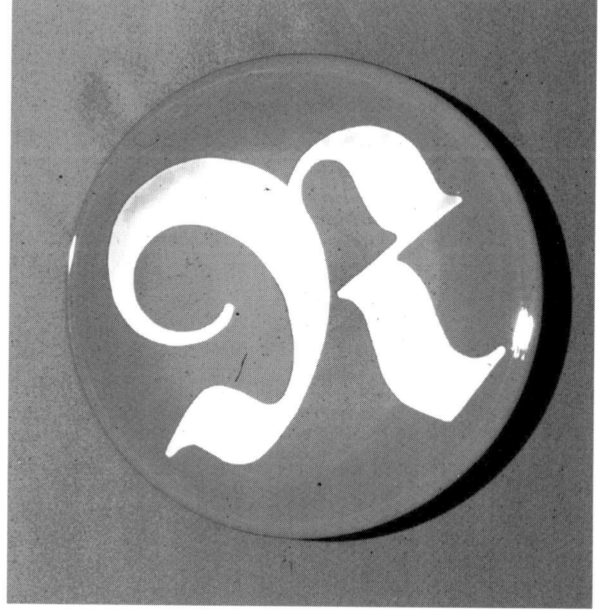

Asa Sandlund: **Fraktur**, 1996
Blown and sandblasted glass, 1 by 18 in. diam.
Courtesy of Vetri International Glass

less challenge our confidence about solid shapes and, like the typography plates, force us to reconsider aspects of the designed environment we take for granted.

Preston Singletary

How is it that so many Pacific Northwest glass artists are making so much work that pays tribute to 20th-century Italian glass? Is it simply because Chihuly's infatuation during his Fulbright year at Venini never wore off? Chihuly wisely kept up his ties to Venice and, by the late 1980s, he embarked on a body of work, the *Venetians* (1988—), that affirmed his roots and further influ-

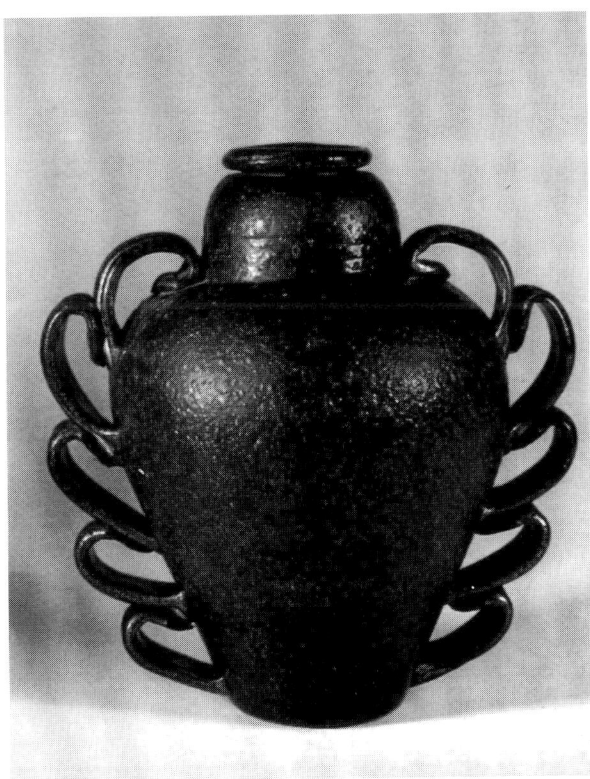

Napoleone Martinuzzi, **Vase**, c. 1928. Glass, 33cm. h. Francesco Carraro collection, Venice, Italy.

enced colleagues like Benjamin Moore (the only one of the group fluent in Italian), and younger artists like Paul Cunningham, Dante Marioni, Janusz Pozniak, and Preston Singletary. By bringing over Italian master glass blowers like Lino Tagliapietra, Pino Signoretto, Loredano Rosin, and Allessandro Diaz de Santillana, Chihuly exposed Pacific Northwest glass artists to complicated procedures and an expanded teamwork concept.

Singletary was part of many of these teams, both at Pilchuk, and at the Lake Union "boathouse" headquarters of Chihuly, Inc. He still continues to work for Benjamin Moore. Helping out the Italians in Seattle, Singletary gained an appreciation both of current working methods and the long history of Italian decorative glass styles. The period Chihuly favored, the so called "interwar years," 1919-1938, had a great impact on all the Seattle converts. Art Deco Italian designers like Napoleone Martinuzzi, Carlo Scarpa, and others working in collaboration before and after World War II with Murano blowers provided the models.

Thus, we see the influence of Martinuzzi on a young glass artist in the *Prestonuzzi Vases* (1996). The link is in the handles elegantly curved and hand applied during the hot shop process. Where Singletary differs from Martinuzzi is in the colors he chooses. Instead of the deep, burnished-appearing colors of the Italian, Singletary uses muted shades of green, orange, red, yellow, and blue. The softer tones give the vases a nostalgic or "retro" look in the *Genies* (1996-97), but the exaggerated necks, the alternating of colored and clear sections, and the differences between the inner and outer wall colors are definitely the younger artist's own contributions.

(Clockwise:)
Asa Sandlund, Preston Singletary,
and Benjamin Moore, Seattle, 1996.
Photo: Russell Johnson

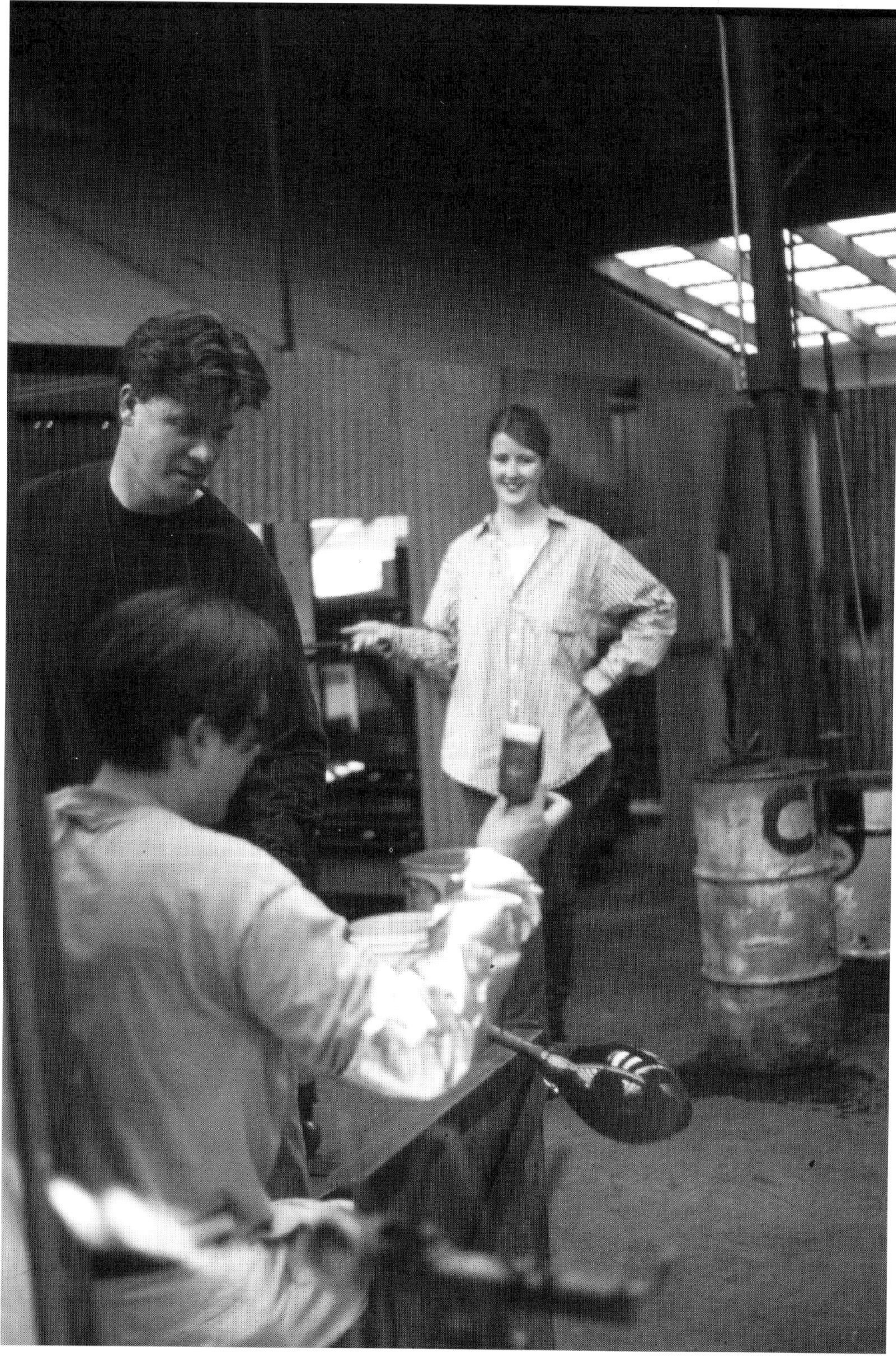

Singletary's experience in Sweden was formative, too. His exposure to the sleek pottery of Swedish designers like Stig Lindberg led to a closer emulation than in Sandlund's abruptly cut and faceted versions. Singletary's *The Genies (Ice Blue)* (1996) reinforces a Swedish feeling with their pale blue colors. With ice blue in relation to white, the three-vase grouping has a Nordic mood.

The Genies (Periwinkle Blue) (1996) use a warmer blue to offset an exploration of red, yellow and green, the "fourth" primary color. All individually blown with clear and colored sections added on the spot, *The Genies* are great technical as well as design accomplishments.

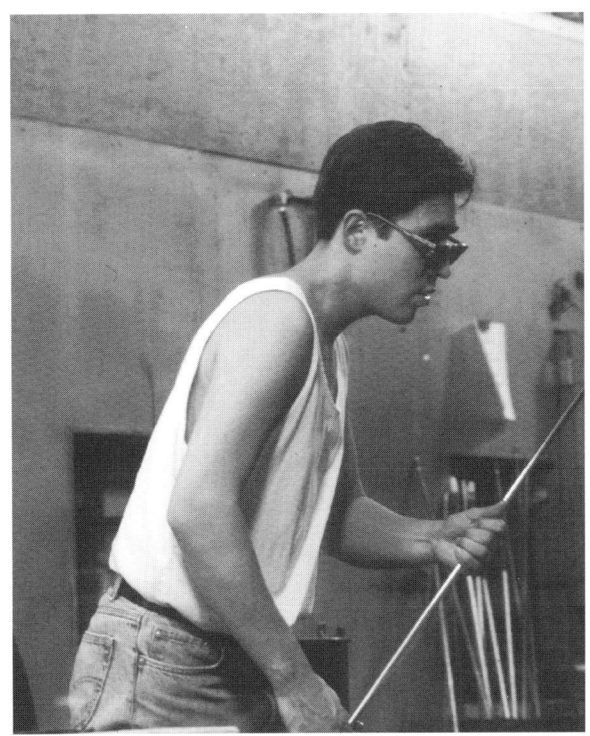

Preston Singletary at Benjamin Moore studios, Seattle, 1994. Photo: Russell Johnson

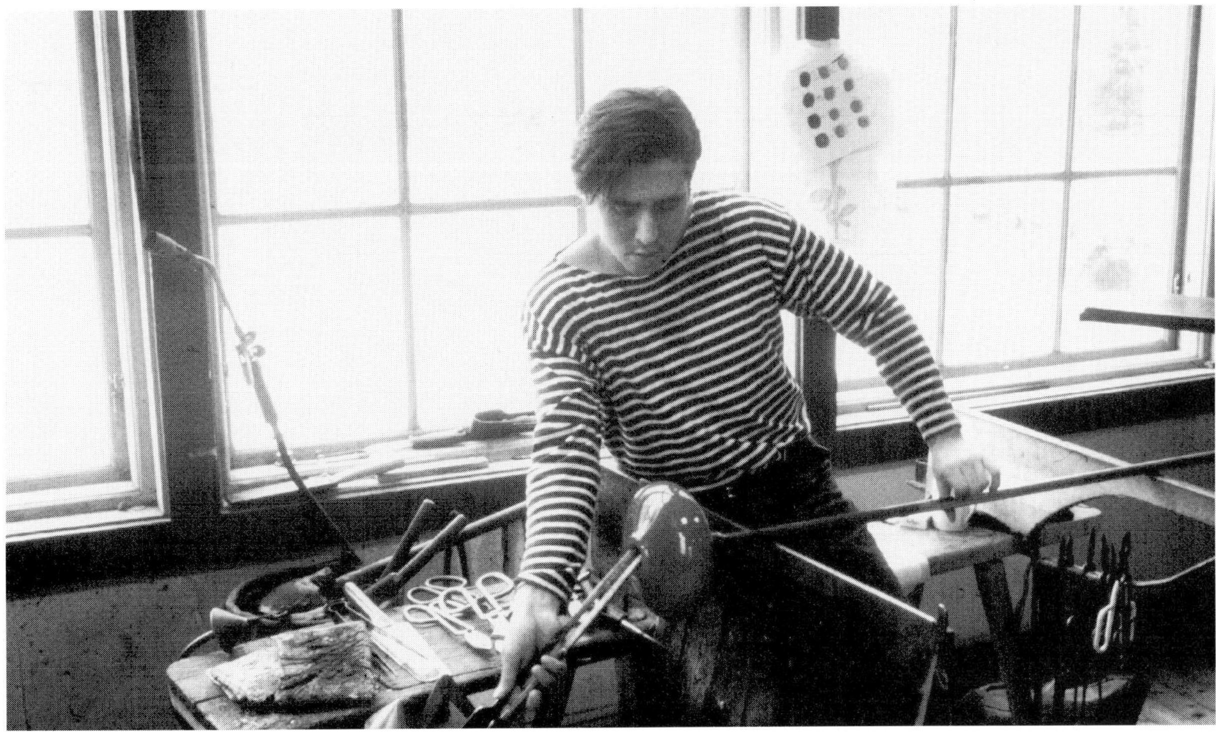

Preston Singletary at Jan-Erik Ritzman's studio, Transjo, Sweden, 1994.

16

Both trios also enact a mock-family grouping of father, mother, and child. Seen in combination with the two *Prestonuzzi Vases, The Genies* take on surprising figurative possibilities.

At an early age in his career, Singletary is already the most well known of all the artists in this exhibition. With invitations and exhibitions in Japan, Europe, and the U.S., Singletary testifies to the growing global language of American studio glass.

At the refined end of high craft, Singletary's and Sandlund's art stand in relief to Hasse's and Koda's. Considered altogether, these four suggest many different directions for other artists interested in glass: design history; exquisite craftsmanship; anti-craft; and the inspiration of nature. It remains to be seen whether the current energy of American studio glass will continue into the coming century. For determined and talented artists like Asa Sandlund and Preston Singletary, Masami Koda and Carl Hasse, anything is possible.

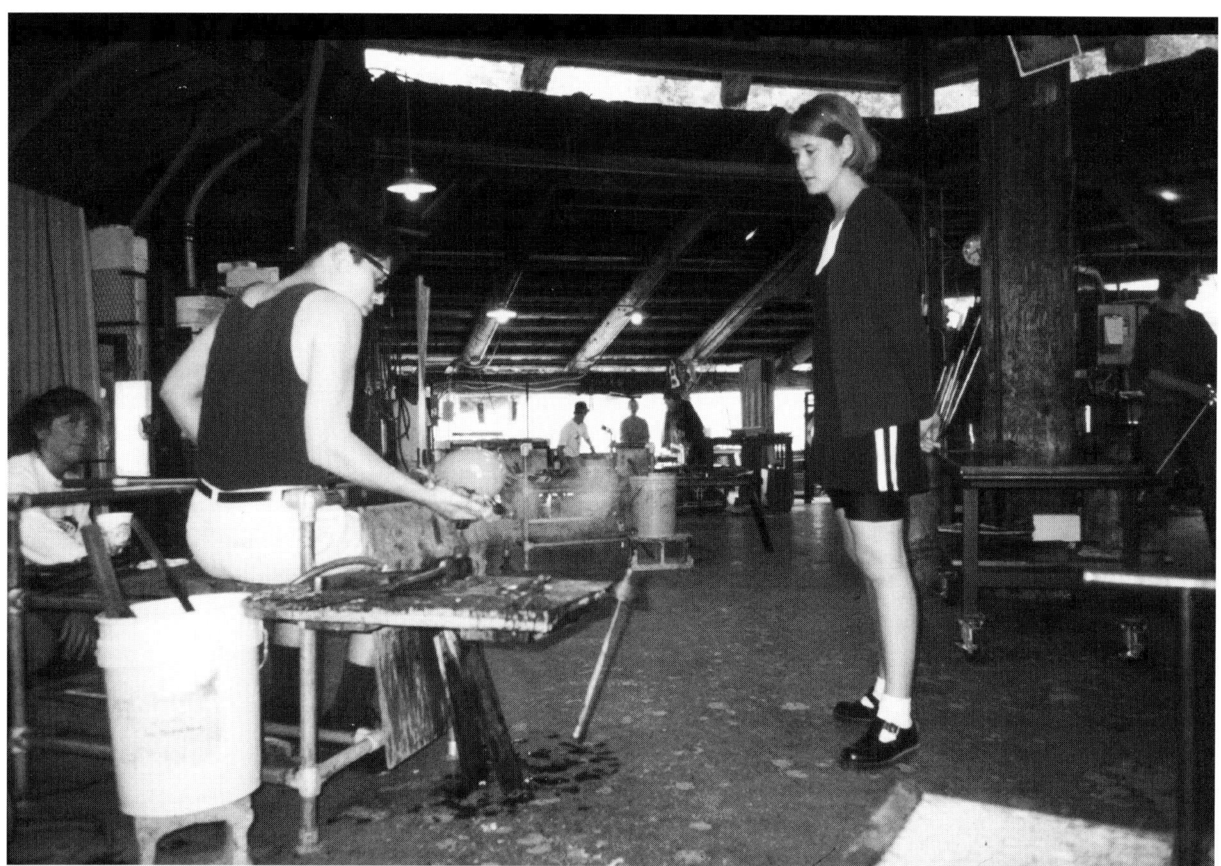

Preston Singletary and Asa Sandlund at Pilchuck Glass School, Stanwood, Washington, 1994.
Photo: Russell Johnson

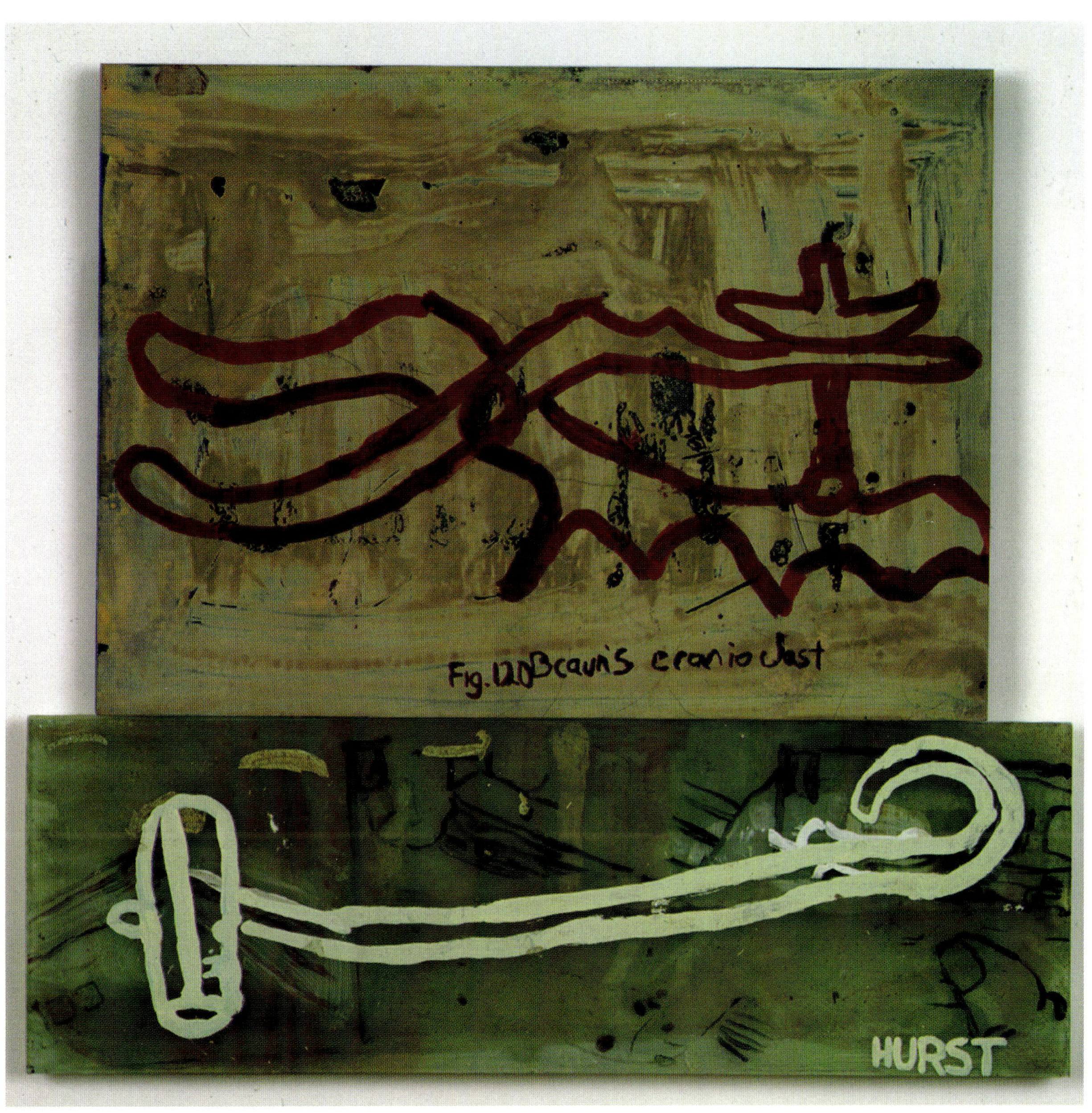

Carl Hasse: **Braun's Craniolast,** 1994
Glass and mixed media, 24 by 24 in.
Courtesy of the artist, Seattle
Photo: Richard Nicol

Carl Hasse: **Car,** 1995
Sandblasted glass and enamel, 18 by 24 in.
Private collection
Photo: Richard Nicol

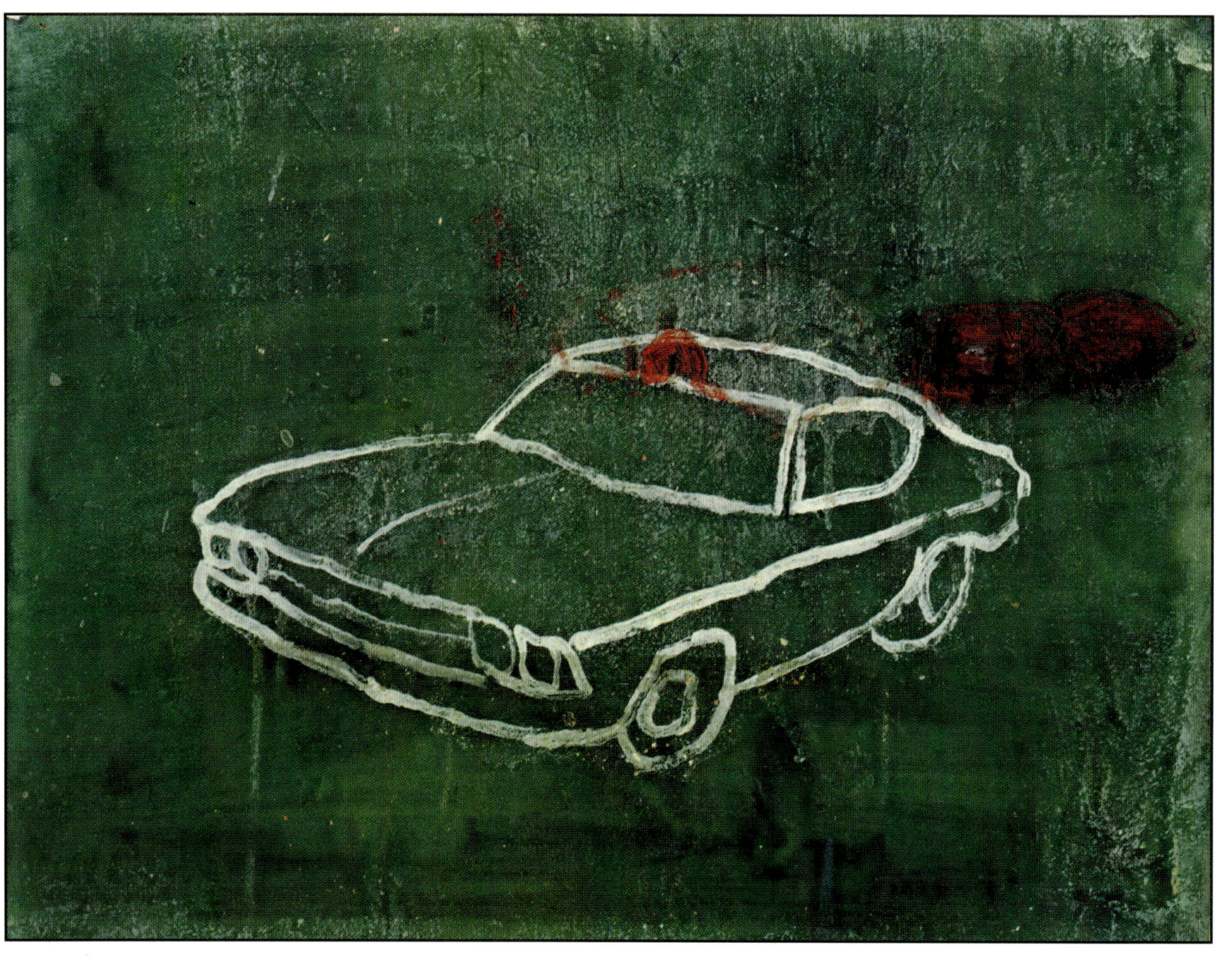

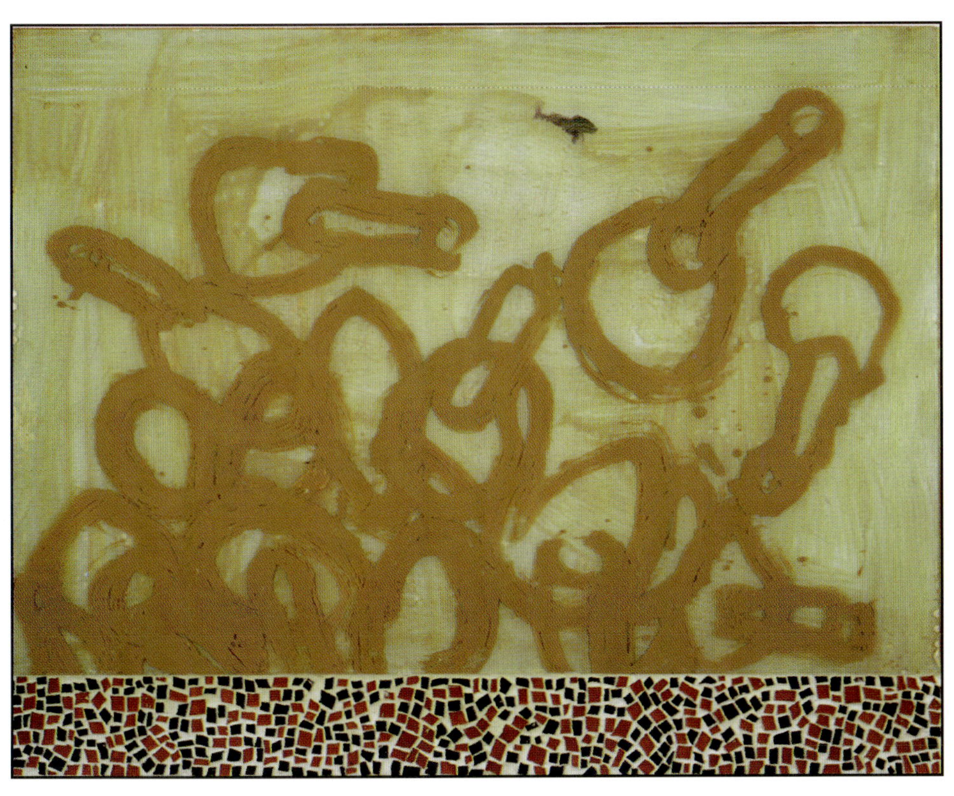

Carl Hasse: **Toolshed,** 1997
Glass mosaic, oil-based enamel on clear glass 28 x 36 in.
Courtesy of the artistPhoto: Richard Nicol

Carl Hasse: **Ouroboros,** 1997
Fired-on enamel on etched glass, painted tin, epoxy, 6 by 14 in.
Courtesy of the artist
Photo: Richard Nicol

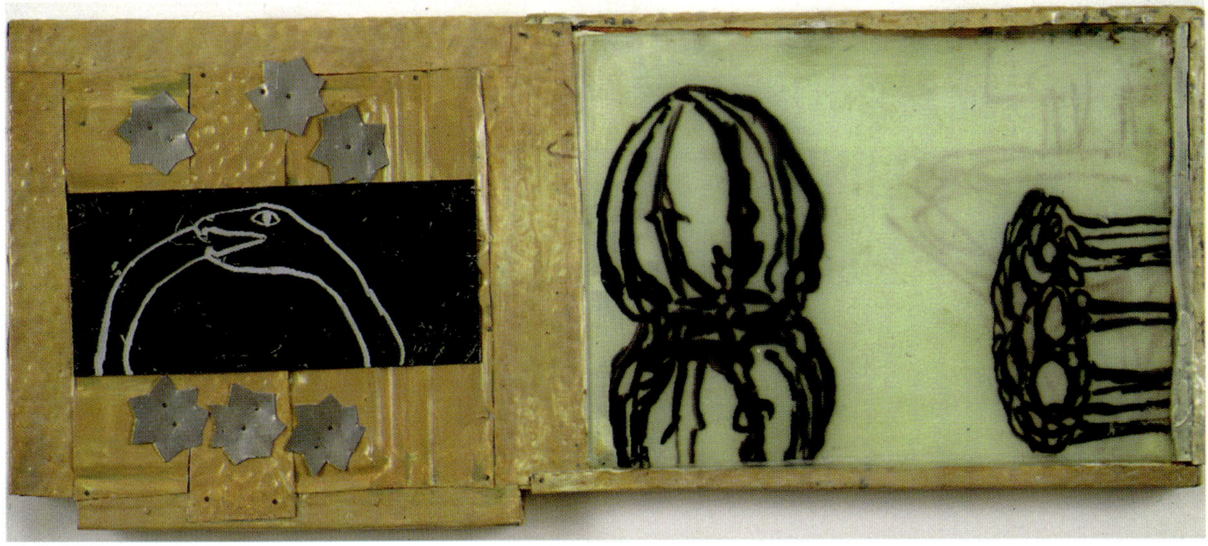

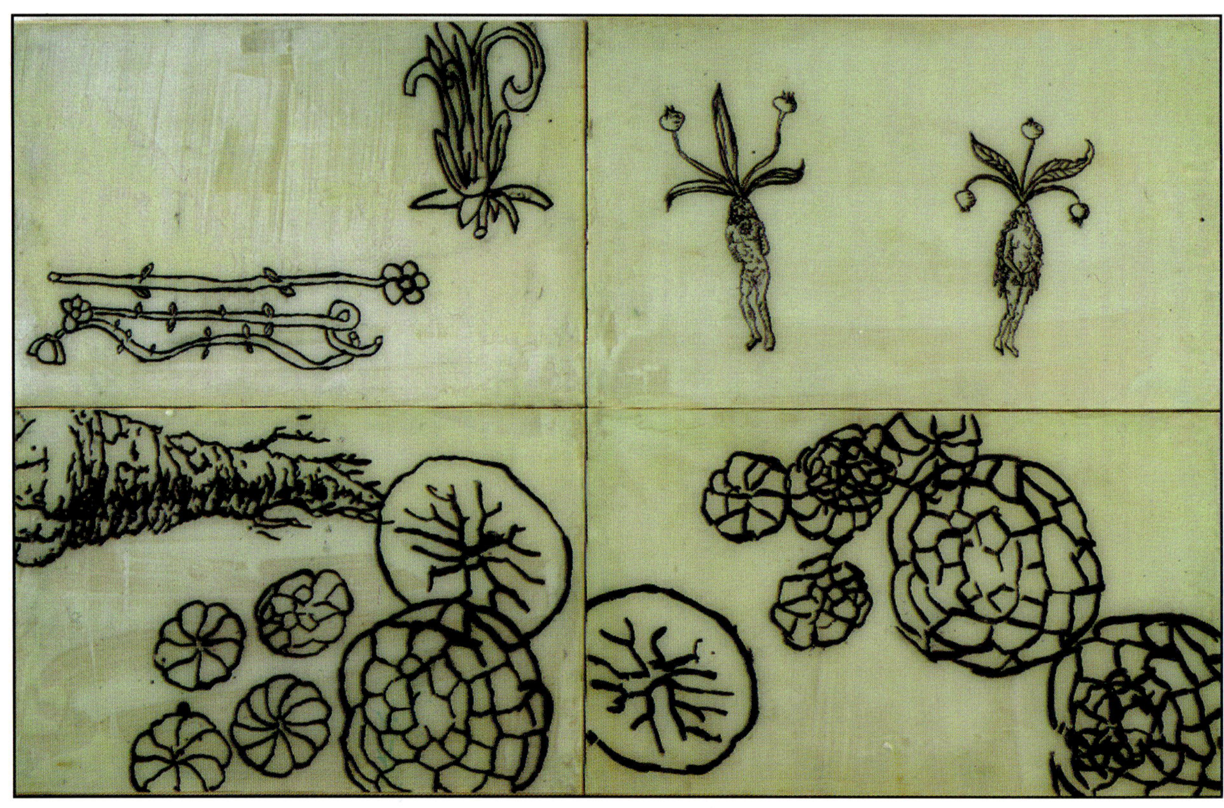

Carl Hasse:
Peyote Buds and Mandrake People, 1997
Fired-on enamel on etched glass,
36 x 58 in.
Courtesy of the artist
Photo: Richard Nicol

Masami Koda:
Departure, 1995
Blown and worked glass, copper oxide with paper and feathers, 17 x16 x7 in.
Courtesy of Vetri International Glass
Photo: Richard Nicol

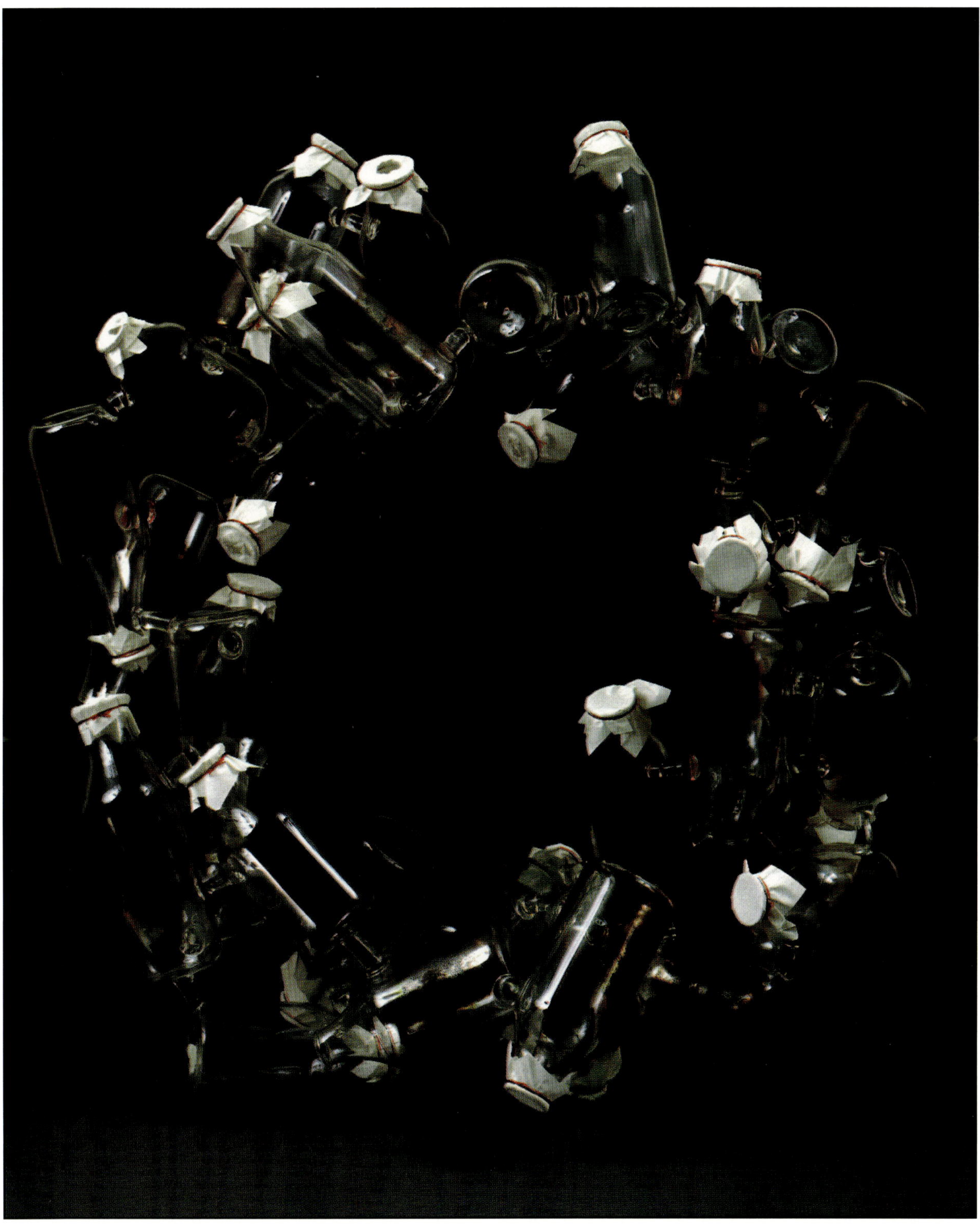

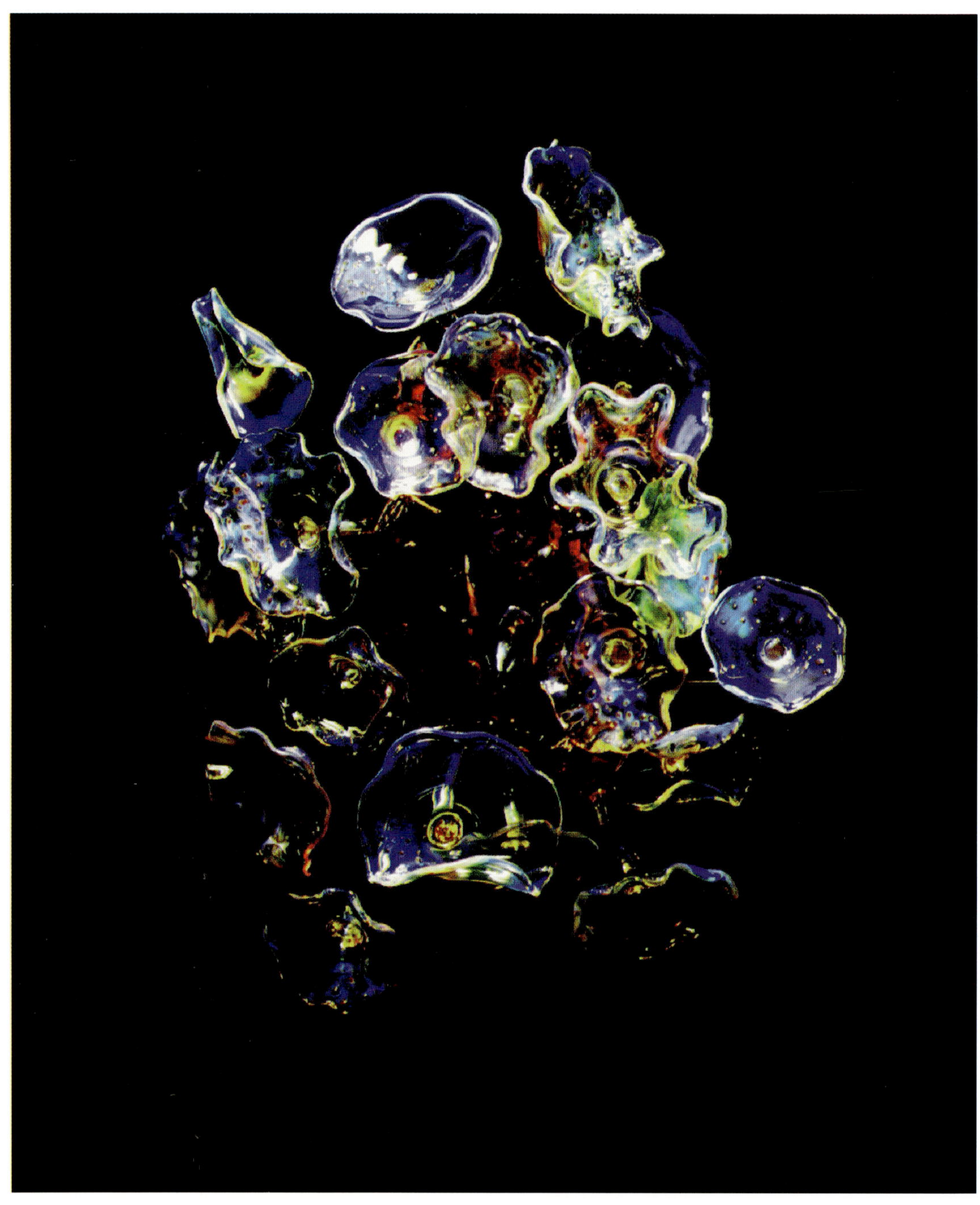

Masami Koda: **200/1 (1-17-95)**, 1995
Lampworked and blown glass with gold paint,
14 by 12 by 6 in.
Courtesy of Vetri International Glass
Photo: Richard Nicol

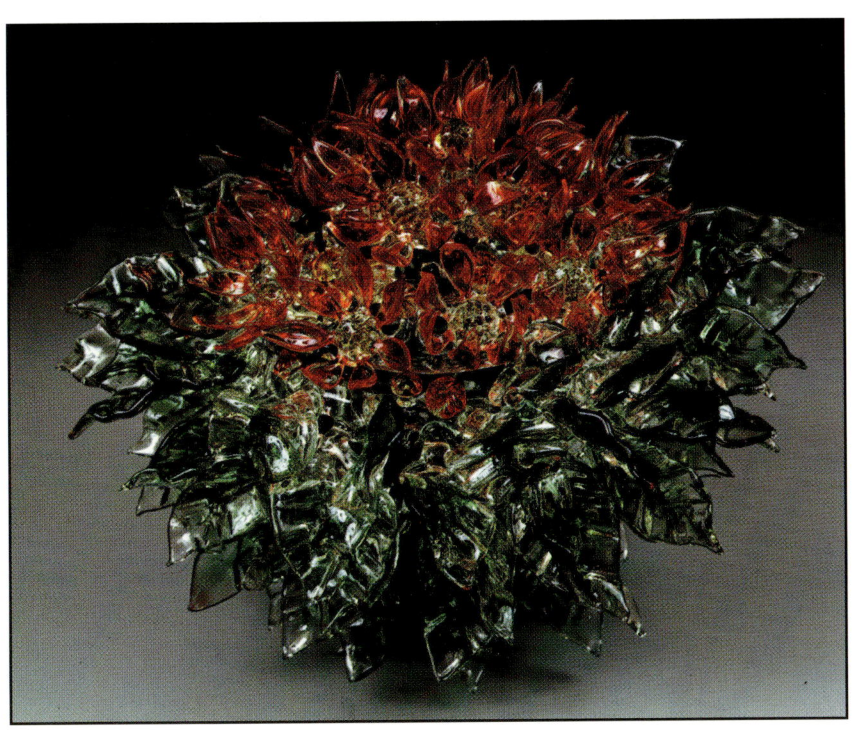

Masami Koda: **Sunflower,** 1995/1997
Lampworked and blown glass, 7 by 10 by 10 in.
Courtesy of Vetri International Glass
Photo: Richard Nicol

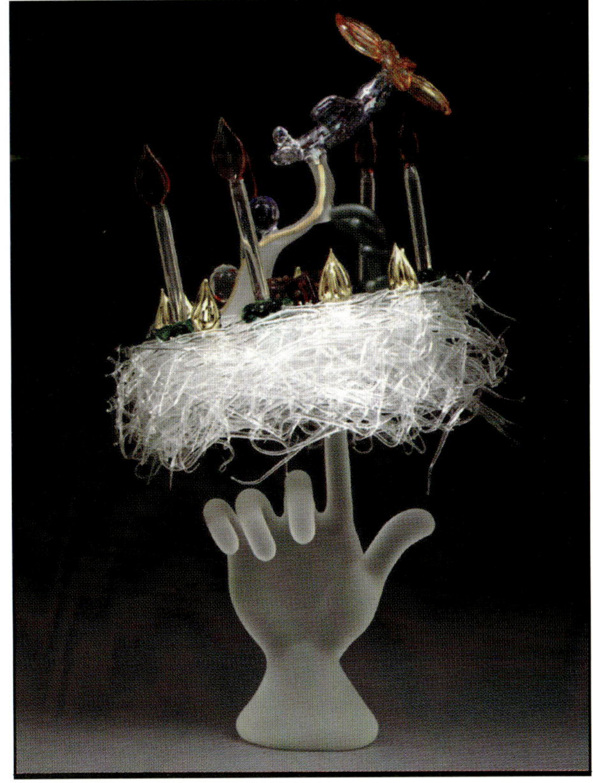

Masami Koda: **Balance**, 1995/97
Lampworked and slumped glass with paint,
11 by 6 by 6 in.
Courtesy of Vetri International Glass
Photo: Richard Nicol

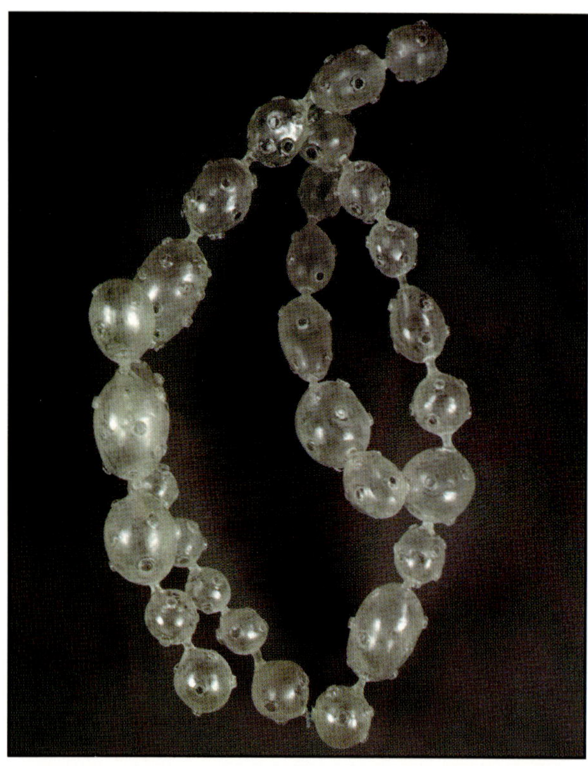

Masami Koda: **Life Force,** 1996
Lampworked and blown glass, 28 by 18 by 6 in.
Courtesy of Vetri International Glass
Photo: Richard Nicol

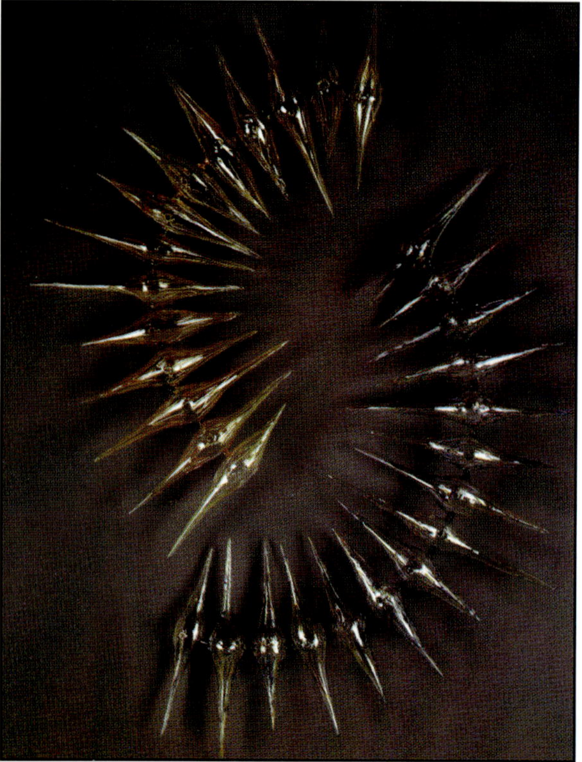

Masami Koda: **Untitled,** 1997
Altered glass tubing with lampworked colored rods,
36 by 26 by 2 in.
Courtesy of Vetri International Glass
Photo: Richard Nicol

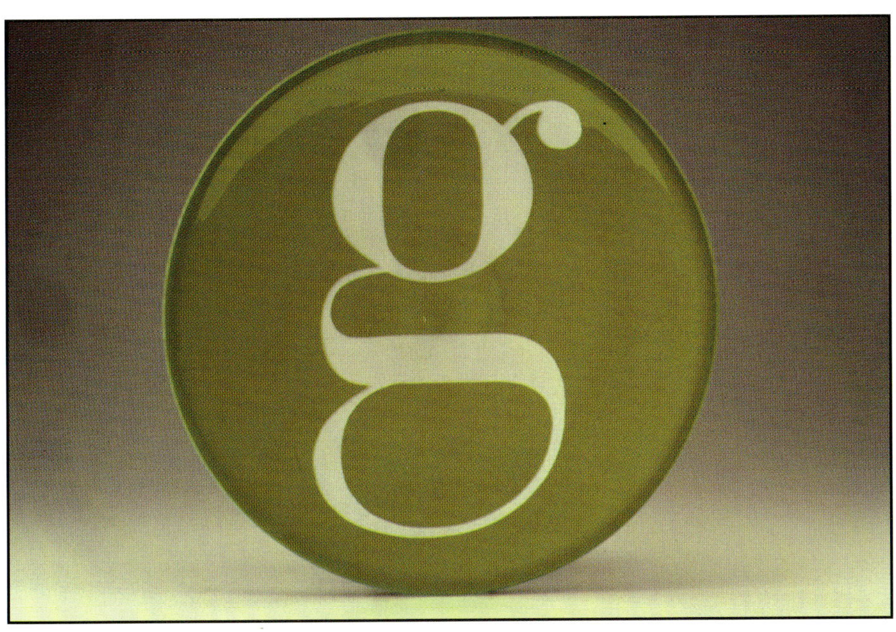

Asa Sandlund: **Bodoni**, 1996
Handblown and sandblasted opaque glass,
2 1/2 by 16 1/2 in. diam.
Courtesy of Vetri International Glass
Photo: Roger Schreiber

Asa Sandlund: **Rockwell,** 1996
Handblown and sandblasted opaque glass
2 1/2 by 16 1/2 in. diam.
Courtesy of Vetri International Glass
Photo: Roger Schreiber

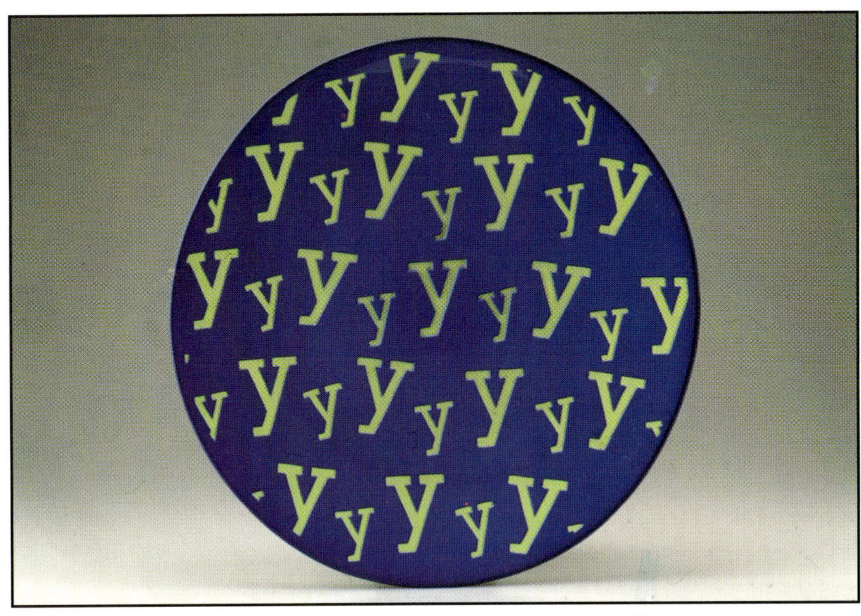

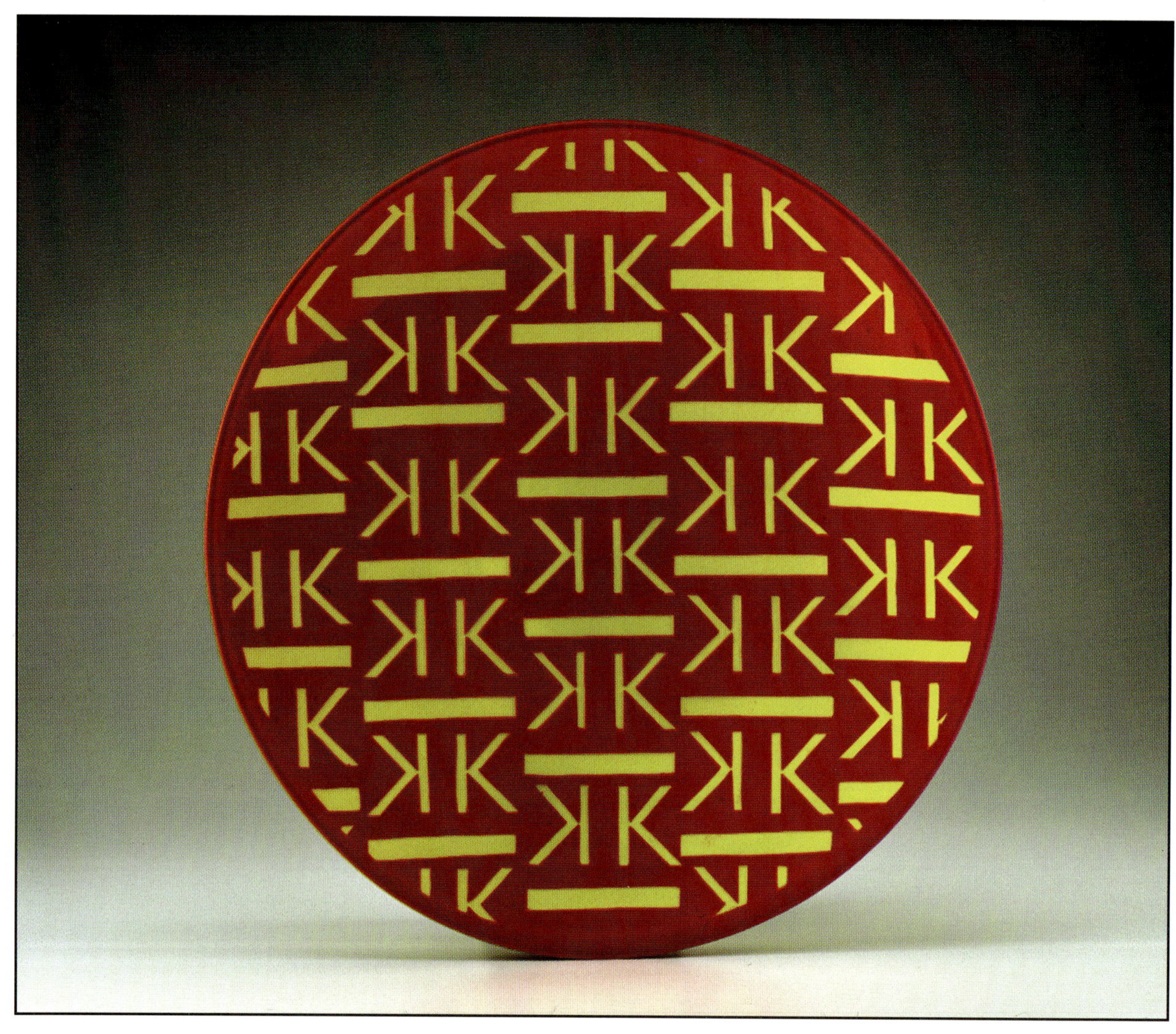

Asa Sandlund: **Frutiger,** 1997
Handblown and sandblasted opaque glass,
2 1/2 x 16 1/2 diam.
Courtesy of Vetri International Glasss
Photo: Roger Schreiber

Asa Sandlund: **Dimensions (Red and Blue),** 1996
Cut and faceted blown glass, 18 x 5 in. diam. each
Courtesy of Vetri International Glass
Photo: Roger Schreiber

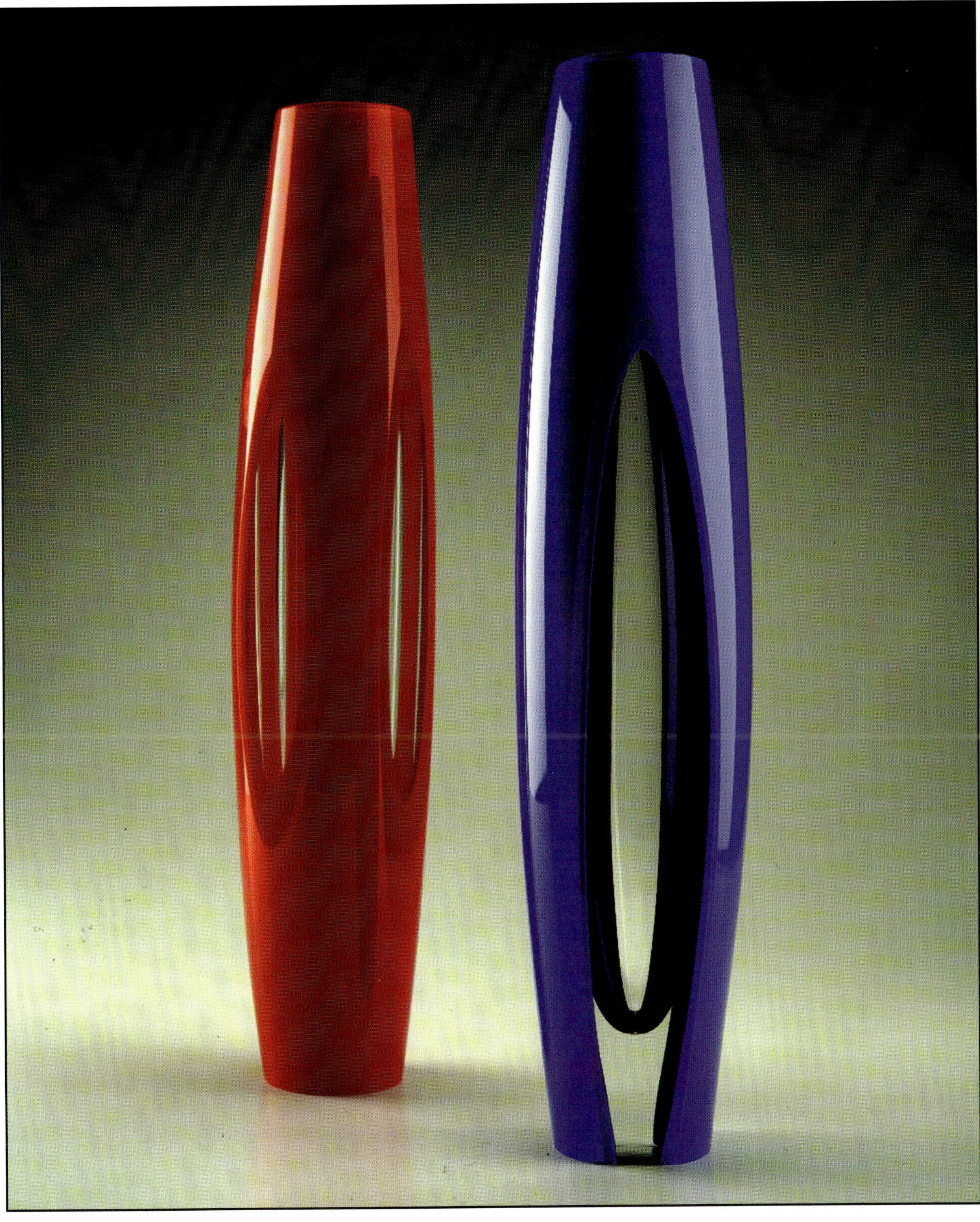

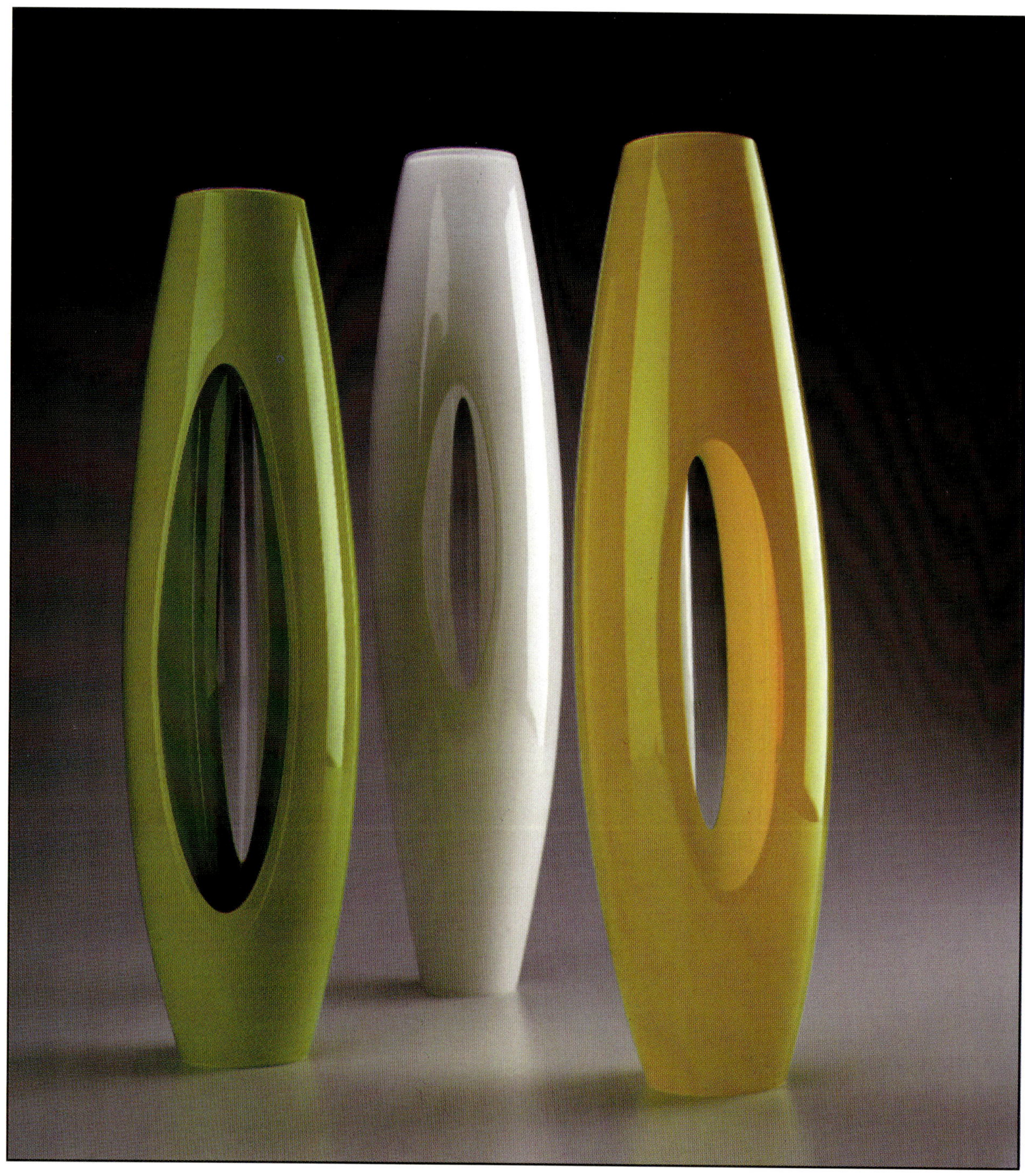

Asa Sandlund: **Dimensions (Yellow, White and Chartreuse),** 1997
Cut and faceted blown glass, 18 x 5 in. diam. each
Courtesy of Vetri International Glass
Photo: Roger Schreiber

Preston Singletary: **Prestonuzzi Pair,** 1996-97
Blown glass, 23 by 12 in. diam.; 8 x 12 in. diam.
Courtesy of William Traver Gallery, Seattle
Photo: Roger Schreiber

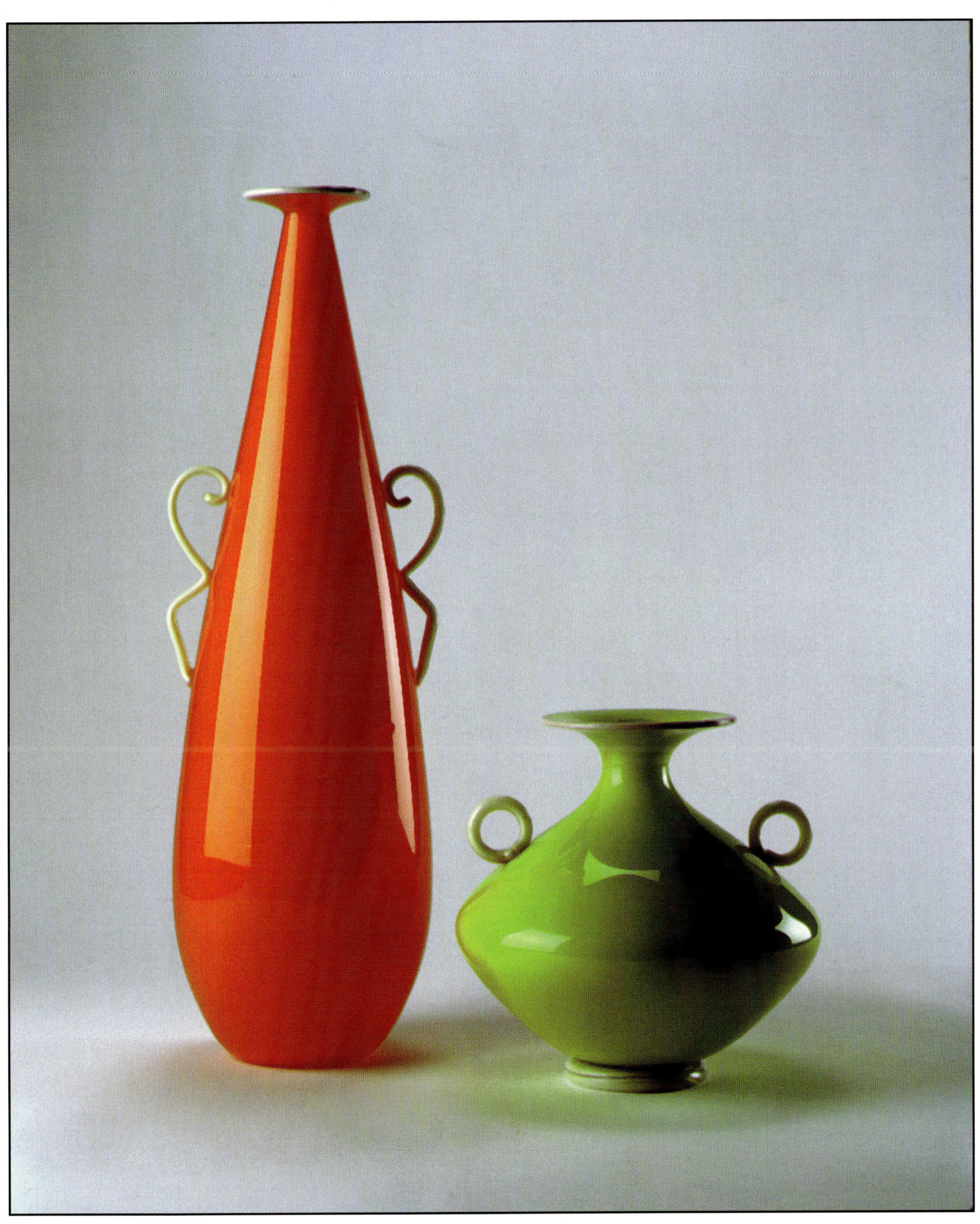

Preston Singletary: **The Genies (Ice Blue),** 1996
Blown glass, 11 1/2 by 10 in. diam.; 17 1/2 by 7 1/2 in. diam.; 19 1/2 by 5 in. diam.
Courtesy of William Traver Gallery
Photo: Roger Schreiber

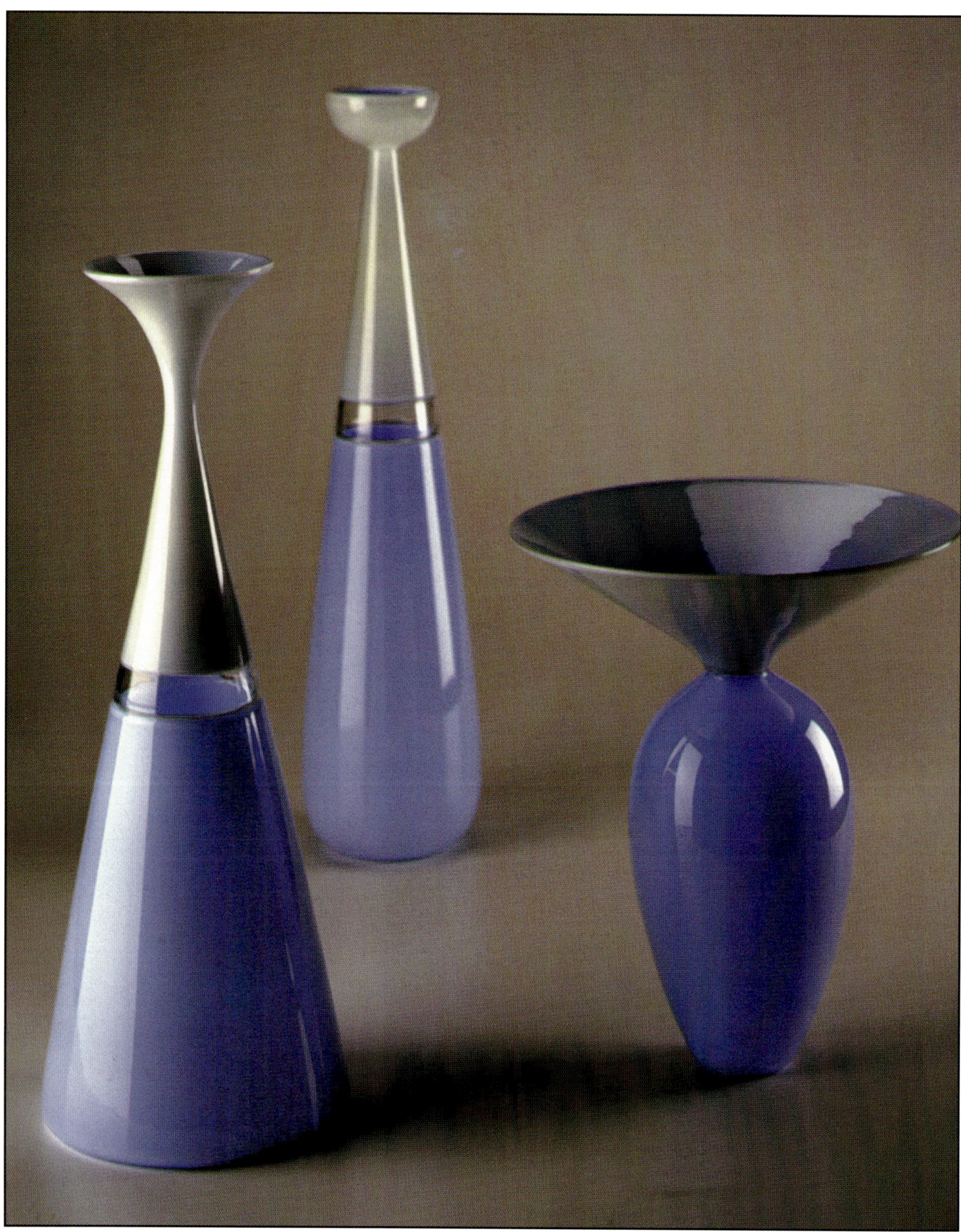

Preston Singletary: **The Genies (Periwinkle Blue),** 1996
Blown glass, 11 1/2 by 8 in. diam.; 18 by 7 in. diam.; 21 by 6 in. diam.
Courtesy of William Traver Gallery
Photo: Roger Schreiber

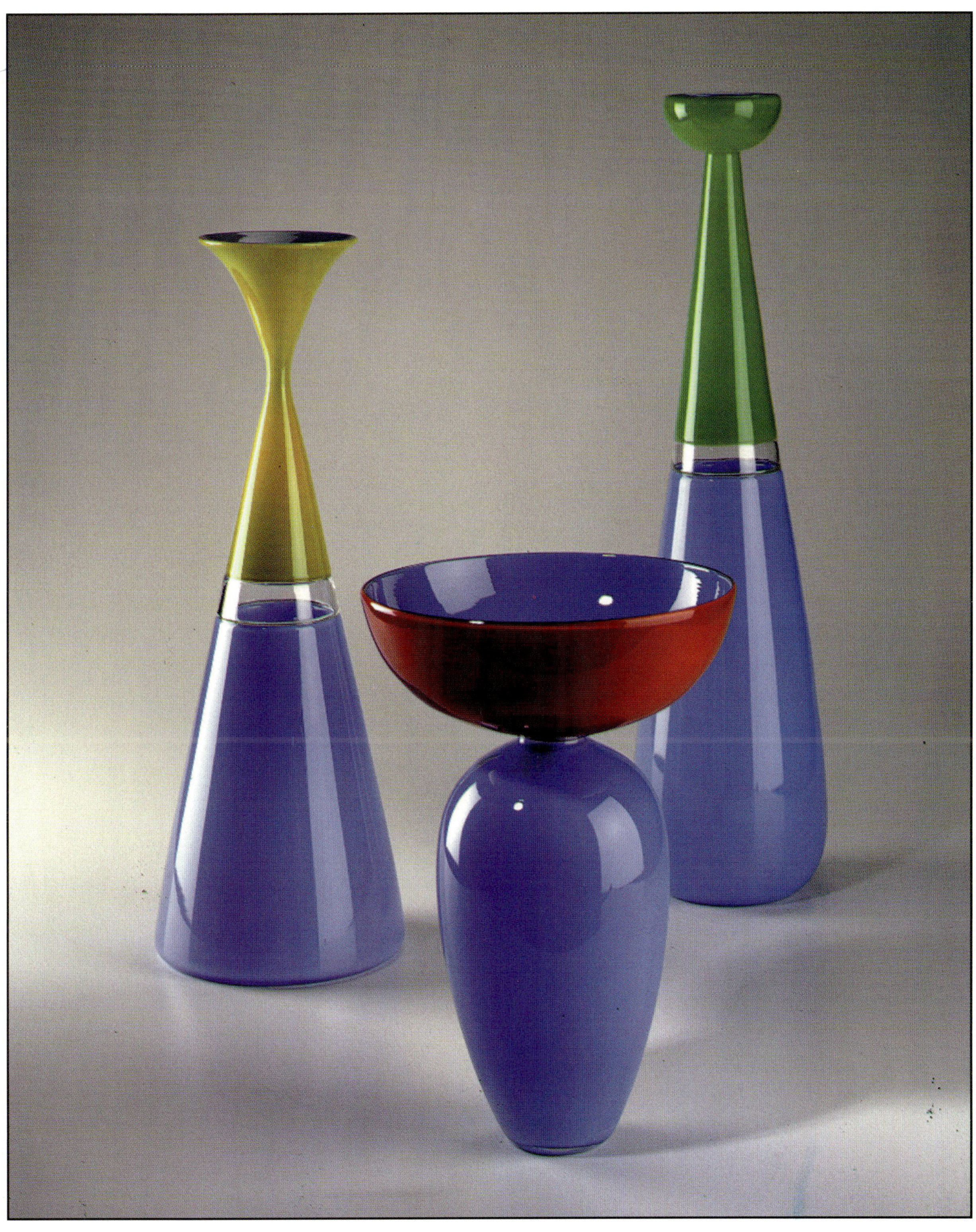

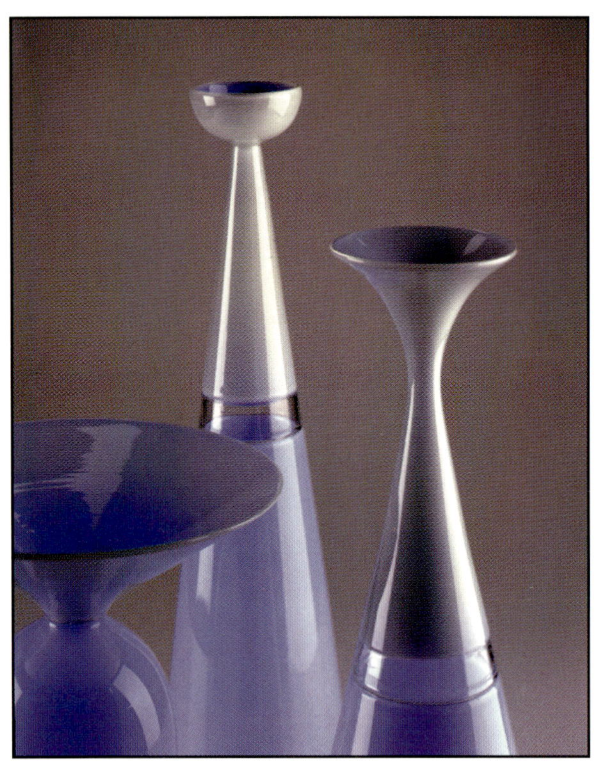

Preston Singletary: **The Genies (Ice Blue) (detail),**
1996
Blown glass, 11 1/2 by 10 in. diam.; 17 1/2 by 7
1/2 in. diam.; 19 1/2 by 5 in. diam.
Courtesy of William Traver Gallery
Photo: Roger Schreiber

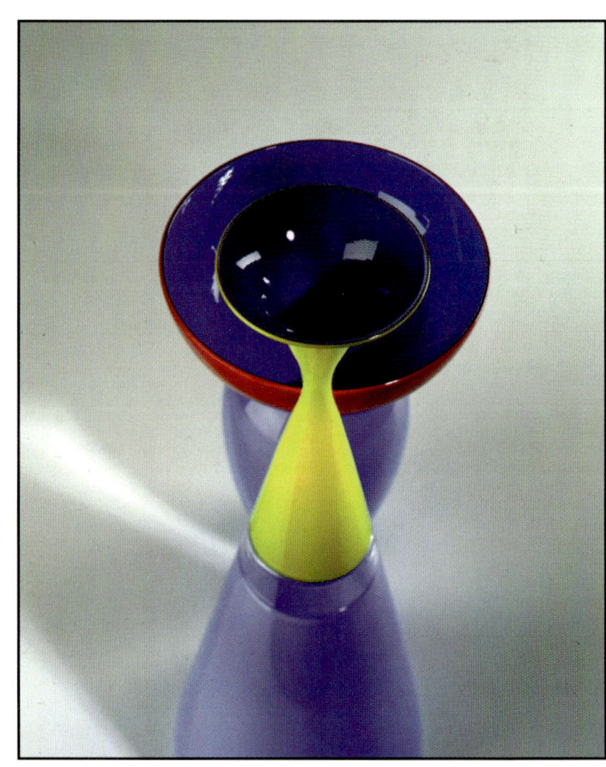

Preston Singletary:
The Genies (Periwinkle Blue), 1996
Blown glass, 11 1/2 by 8 in. diam.; 18 by 7 in.
diam.; 21 by 6 in. diam.
Courtesy of William Traver Gallery
Photo: Roger Schreiber

BIOGRAPHIES

Carl Hasse, 1997, Photo: Douglas Tucker

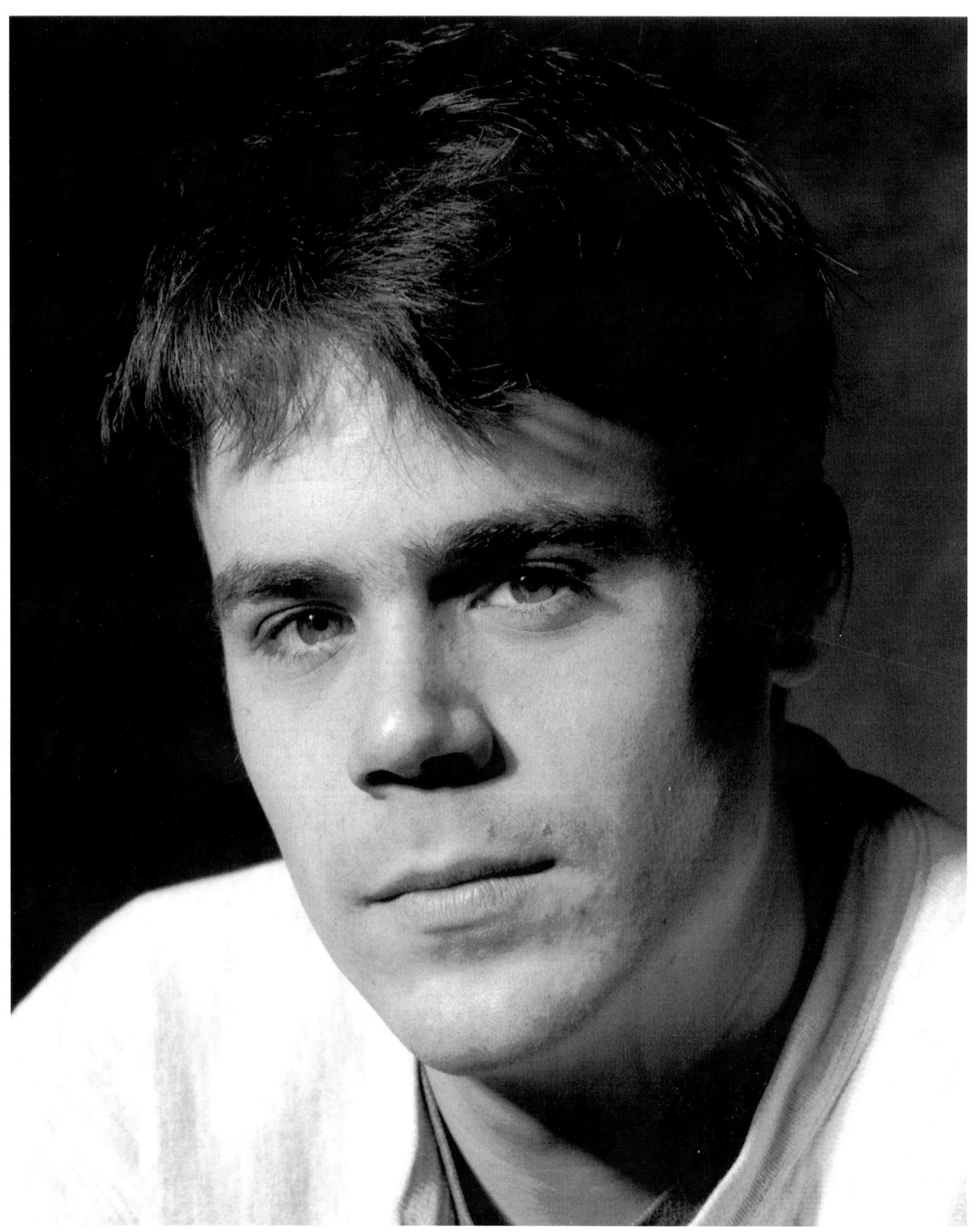

Carl Hasse (b. 1971)

Education

1996   Pilchuck Glass School, Stanwood, Washington
1993   B.F.A., Alfred University, Alfred, New York
       Emerging Artist in Residence, Pilchuck Glass School
1992   Rhode Island School of Design, Providence, Rhode Island
1991   Haystack Mountain School of Crafts, Deer Isle, Maine

Selected Exhibitions

1997   *Four in Glass,* FOVA Galleries, Texas Tech University,   Lubbock, Texas
1996   *Carl Hasse,* Bubba Mavis Gallery, Seattle
       O.K. Hotel, Seattle
1995   *Abstraction=Representation,* Open Space, Victoria, British Columbia, Canada
       (Matthew Kangas, curator)
1994   *The Beauty of Painted Glass: New Directions in the Northwest,* Bellevue Art Museum,
       Bellevue, Washington, (Erika Michael, curator)
1993   *In the Woods.../A Group Exhibition by the 1993 Emerging Artists in Residence at
       Pilchuck Glass School,* Elliott Brown Gallery, Seattle

Masami Koda, 1997, Photo: Douglas Tucker

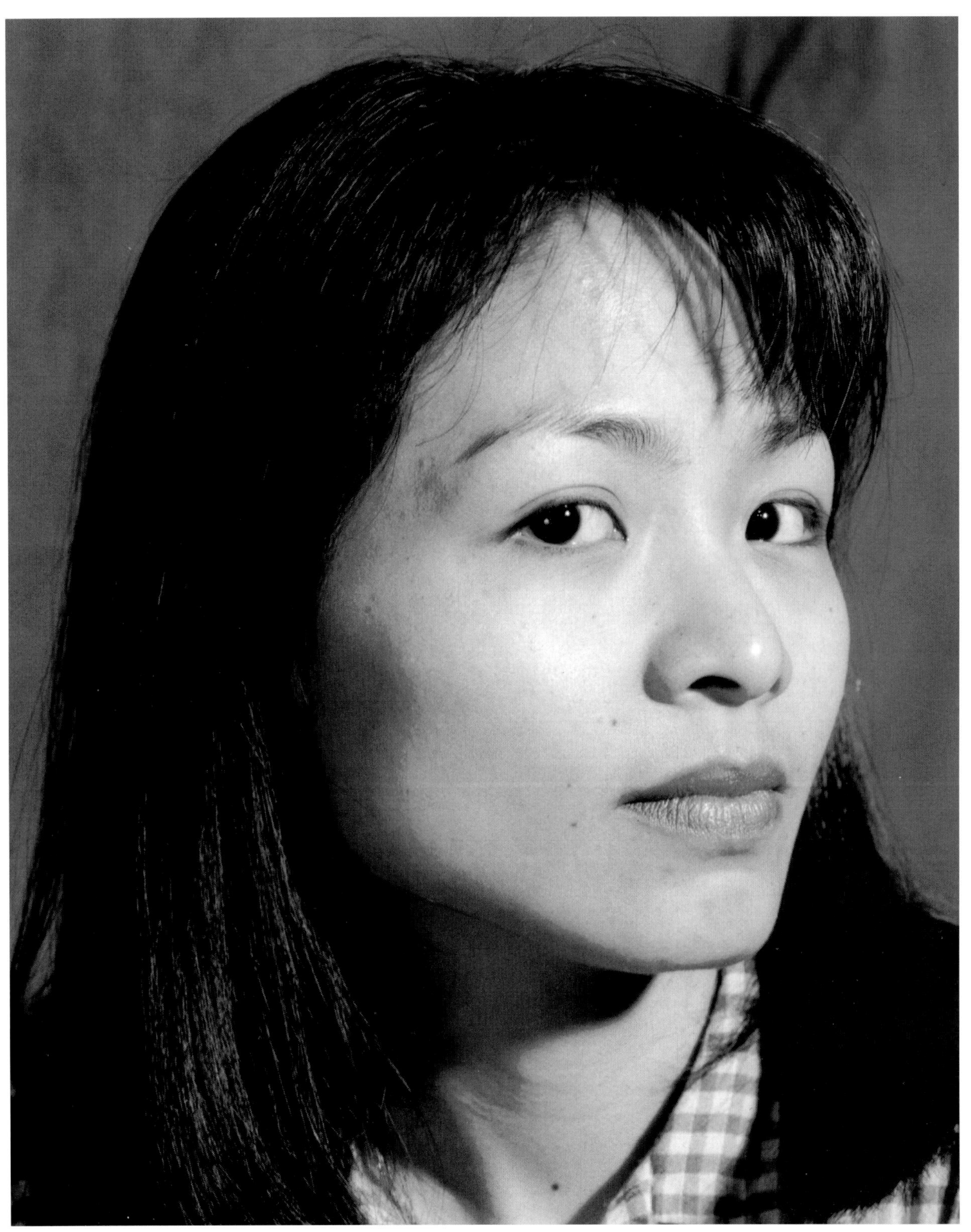

Masami Koda, 1997, Photo: Douglas Tucker

Masami Koda (b. 1966)

Education

1994   M.F.A., Alfred University, Alfred, New York
            Pilchuck Glass School
1989-1992   Cleveland Institute of Art, Cleveland, Ohio
1989   B.F.A., Osaka University of the Arts, Osaka, Japan
            Certificate of Museum Studies, Osaka University of the Arts

Selected Exhibitions

1997   *Four in Glass,* FOVA Galleries, Texas Tech University
            Vetri International Glass, Seattle
1996   *Figurative Small Works,* Armory Art Center, West Palm
            Beach, Florida (Bruce Helander, juror)
            Glasshouse Gallery, Seattle
            Margo Jacobsen Gallery, Portland, Oregon
1995   *23rd Annual International Glass Exhibition,* Habatat
            Galleries, Pontiac, Michigan
1994   *Pilchuck Glass School Exhibition,* Seattle-Tacoma
            International Airport
1989   Daigakudo Gallery, Osaka, Japan
            Museum of Modern Art, Hyogo, Japan

Selected Collections

Keiko Akiyama, Long Beach, California
Maureen Ellison, Seattle
Jill Pelisek, Milwaukee, Wisconsin
Denise Pelletier, New York
Pilchuck Glass School
Scottsdale Center for the Arts, Scottsdale, Arizona
William and Anne Traver, Seattle
Represented by Vetri International Glass, Seattle, and Habatat Galleries, Pontiac, Michigan.

Asa Sandlund, 1997, Photo: Roger Schreiber

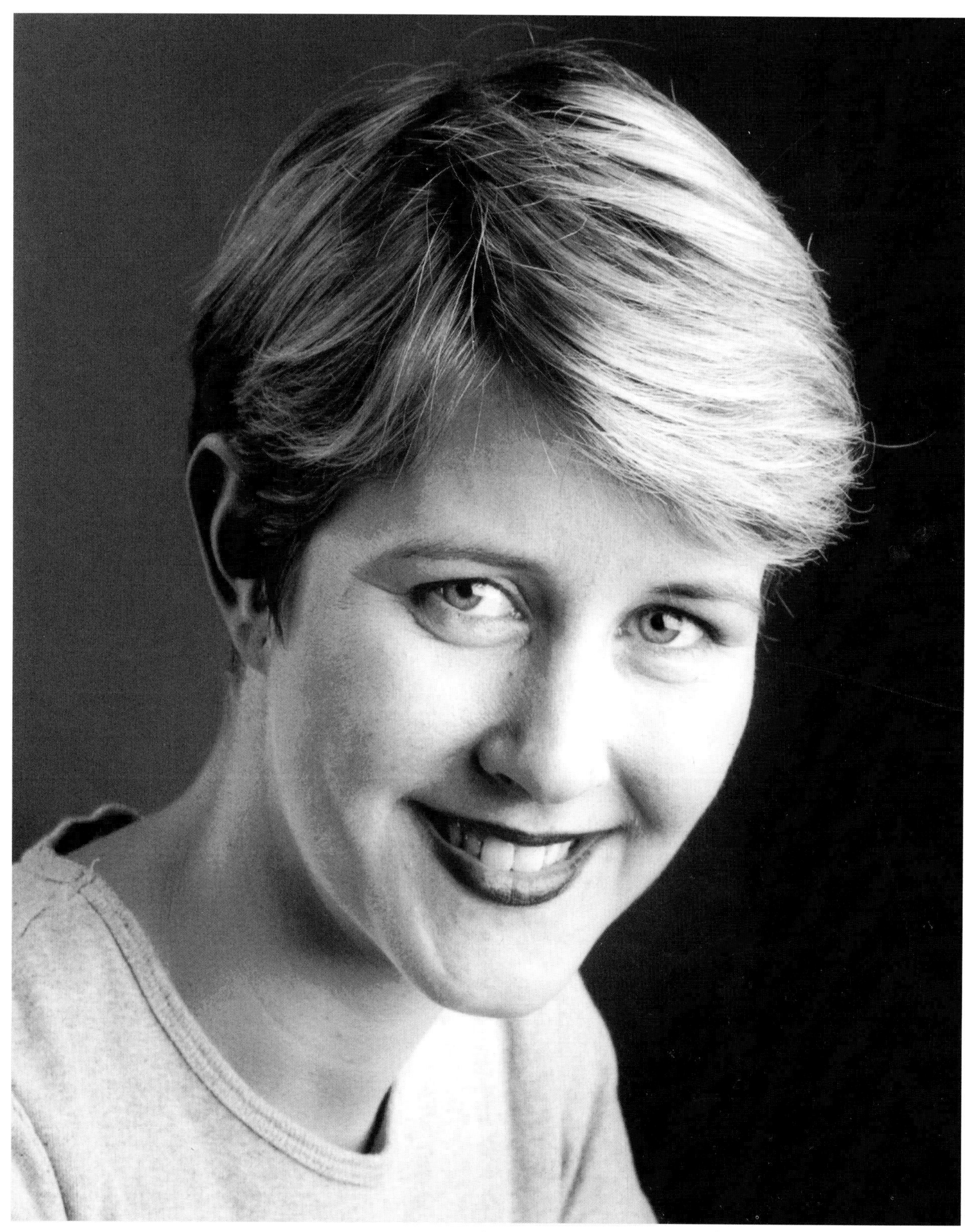

Asa Sandlund (b. 1969)

Education

1994	B.A., Beckmans School of Design, Stockholm
	Pilchuck Glass School
1990	Phalmans Marketing Institute, Stockholm
1989	Ecole des Beaux-Arts, Paris, France
1987	Magdalene Hall College, Oxford, England

Selected Exhibitions

1997	*Four in Glass,* FOVA Galleries, Texas Tech University, Lubbock, Texas
	Vetri International Glass, Seattle
1994	*Objects on the Table,* Ahlens Department Store, Stockholm
1993	Millesgarden, Stockholm
1992	*Today's Package Design,* Culture Museum, Stockholm

Selected Collections

Ahlens Department Store, Stockholm
Judy and Grant Beck, Mercer Island, Washington
Margo and Warren Coville, Bloomfield Hills, Michigan
Sonja Blomdahl and Dick Weiss, Seattle
FGH, Stockholm
Lowe Brindfors, Stockholm
Pilchuck Glass School
Poe Form, Stockholm
Represented by Vetri International Glass, Seattle

Preston Singletary, 1997, Photo: Roger Schreiber

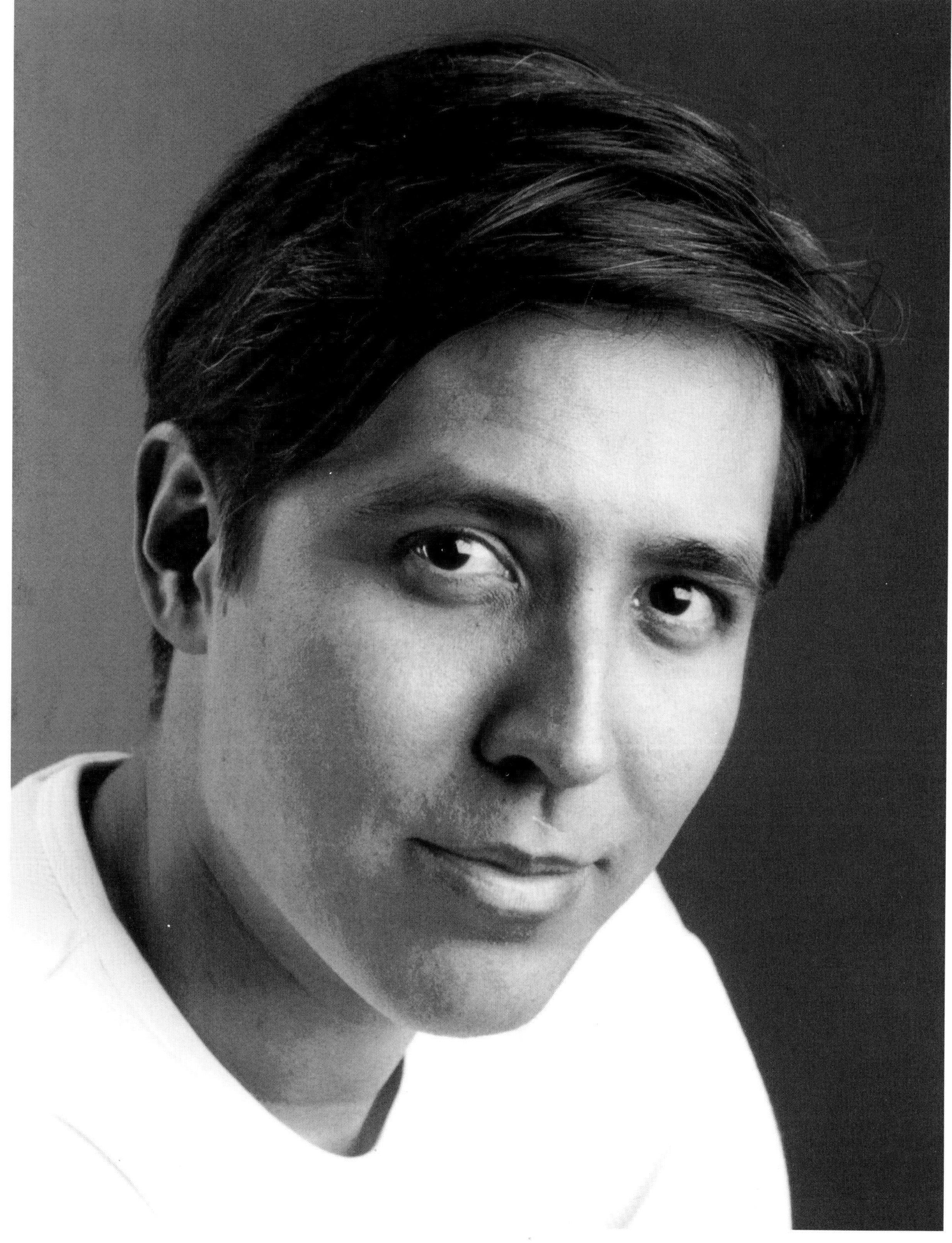

Preston Singletary (b. 1963)

Education

1984-87   Pilchuck Glass School (studied with Dan Dailey; Benjamin Moore; Lino Tagliapietra)
1981   Lincoln High School, Seattle

Selected Exhibitions

1997   *Four in Glass,* FOVA Galleries, Texas Tech University, Lubbock, Texas
           Preston Singletary: Northwest Coast Designs in Glass, Vetri International Glass
           Kiva Fine Arts, Santa Fe, New Mexico
           Gump's, San Francisco
           Margo Jacobsen Gallery, Portland, Oregon
1996   *A New Generation: Preston Singletary, Paul Cunningham, and Janusz Pozniak,*
           William Traver Gallery, Seattle
1995   Leedy-Voulkos Galleries, Kansas City, Missouri
1994   *16th Annual International Pilchuck Glass School Exhibition,* William Traver Gallery
1993   Margo Jacobsen Gallery, Portland, Oregon
           Susan Duvall Gallery, Aspen, Colorado
           Preston Singletary, Maggio Gallery, New Orleans, Louisiana
1992   *New Visions,* Visual Arts Center of Alaska, Anchorage
1991   *Preston Singletary,* The Glass Gallery, Bethesda, Maryland
           The Americans: A Venetian Tradition, West End Gallery,
           Corning, New York (Kate Elliott and William Warmus, co-curators)
           Gallery Nakama, Tokyo, Japan
1990   Maurine Littleton Gallery, Washington, DC
           Kurland Summers Gallery, Washington, DC
           Seibu Department Store, Tokyo, Japan
1989   *11th Annual International Pilchuck Glass School Exhibition,* William Traver Gallery
1986   Hundredwaters Gallery, Seattle

Selected Collections

Sonja Blomdahl and Dick Weiss, Seattle
Lowe Brindfors, Stockholm
Handelsbanken, Stockholm
Anne Gould Hauberg, Seattle
Susie and Hiro Hino, Woodinville, Washington
C. David Hughbanks, Seattle

Benjamin Moore, Seattle
Museum of Natural History, Anchorage, Alaska
Group Health Cooperative of Puget Sound, Seattle
Jon and Mary Shirley, Medina, Washington
Represented by William Traver Gallery and
Vetri International Glass

Selected Bibliography

Carl Hasse

Matthew Kangas, *Four in Glass*. Lubbock, TX: FOVA Galleries, Texas Tech University, 1997.

Yvonne Owen, "Abstraction=Representation: Elements of Surprise," *Reflex,* February, 1996.

Yvonne Owen, "Curatorial Concerns: Three Victoria Shows," *Artichoke,* Spring, 1996.

Masami Koda

Matthew Kangas, *Four in Glass*. Lubbock, TX: FOVA Galleries, Texas Tech University, 1997.

Gary Schwan, "Armory's small works exhibit runs to mid-June," *Palm Beach Post*, May 10, 1996

Asa Sandlund

Matthew Kangas, *Four in Glass*. Lubbock, TX: FOVA Galleries, Texas Tech University, 1997.

Lotta Lewenhaupt, *Elle Decor* (Swedish edition), September, 1996.

Camilla Berggren, "The nicest exhibition in Beckman's history?...," *Embryo* (Sweden), June, 1994.

Lage Stone, "Advertising, graphic design and glass design is the challenge for the young Asa Sandlund...," *Skona Hem* (Sweden), June, 1994.

Rebecka Traschys, "Form...," *Svenska Dagbladet* (Sweden), May 20, 1994.

Lisbeth Borger-Bendegard, "Asa Sandlund shows glass plates from the typography world," *Svenska Dagbladet* (Sweden), May 25, 1994.

Preston Singletary

Marie Gray, "Alligator Goblets," *Best International* #5 (Japan), May, 1991.

Matthew Kangas, *Four in Glass*. Lubbock, TX: FOVA Galleries, Texas Tech University, 1997.

"Preston Singletary: Portfolio," *Glasswork* #7 (Japan), December, 1990.

Robin Updike, "Many nurturing artworks of varied media showing this month in Seattle galleries," *The Seattle Times* Tempo, March 14, 1996.

——————, "Artist Preston Singletary blew the glasss globes that cover the soft lights...," *The Seattle Times*, March 30, 1997.

Geoff Wichert, "A New Generation: Preston Singletary, Paul Cunningham, and Janusz Pozniak," *GLASS* #64, Fall, 1996.

Dick Weiss, "The Glassblowers of the Pacific Northwest," *Glasswork* #11 (Japan), March, 1992.

Checklist of the Exhibition

Height precedes width precedes depth.
All dimensions are in inches.

Carl Hasse

Braun's Craniolast, 1994
Glass and mixed media, 24 by 24 in.
Courtesy of the artist, Seattle

Car, 1995
Sandblasted glass and enamel, 18 by 24 in.
Private collection

Forest Pine, 1997
Glass mosaic with acrylic on paper, 39 by 28
in.
Courtesy of the artist

Ouroboros, 1997
Fired-on enamel on etched glass, painted tin,
epoxy,
6 by 14 in.
Courtesy of the artist

Peyote Buds and Mandrake People, 1997
Fired-on enamel on etched glass, 36 by 58 in.
Courtesy of the artist

Toolshed, 1997
Glass mosaic, oil-based enamel on clear
stained glass, 28 by 36 in.
Courtesy of the artist

Masami Koda

Hands with Hope, 1994/1997
Lampworked glass and paint, 5 by 4 by 2 in. each
Courtesy of Vetri International Glass, Seattle

Departure, 1995
Blown and worked glass, copper oxide with
paper and feathers, 17 by 16 by 7 in.
Courtesy of Vetri International Glass

200/1 (1-17-95), 1995
Lampworked and blown glass with gold paint,
14 by 12 by 6 in.
Courtesy of Vetri International Glass

Balance, 1995/1997
Lampworked and slumped glass with paint, 11
by 6 by 6 in.
Courtesy of Vetri International Glass

Sunflower, 1995/1997
Lampworked and blown glass, 7 by 10 by 10 in.
Courtesy of Vetri International Glass

Life Force, 1996
Lampworked and blown glass, 28 by 18 by 6
in.
Courtesy of Vetri International Glass

Untitled, 1997
Altered glass tubing with lampworked colored
rods,
36 by 26 by 2 in.
Courtesy of Vetri International Glass

Asa Sandlund

Rockwell, 1997
Handblown and sandblasted opaque glass, 2 1/2 by 16 1/2 in. diam.
Courtesy of Vetri International Glass

Bodoni, 1997
Handblown and sandblasted opaque glasss, 3 by 16 1/2 in. diam.
Courtesy of Vetri International Glass

Frutiger, 1997
Handblown and sandblasted opaque glass, 2 1/2 by 16 1/2 diam.
Courtesy of Vetri International Glass

Dimensions (Red and Blue), 1997
Cut and faceted blown glass, 18 by 5 in. diam. each
Courtesy of Vetri International Glass

Dimensions (Yellow, White and Chartreuse), 1997
Cut and faceted blown glass, 18 by 5 in. diam. each
Courtesy of Vetri International Glass

Preston Singletary

Prestonuzzi Pair, 1996-97
Blown glass, 23 by 12 in. diam.; 8 by 12 in. diam.
Courtesy of William Traver Gallery, Seattle

The Genies (Ice Blue), 1996
Blown glass, 11 1/2 by 10 in. diam.; 17 1/2 by 7 1/2 in. diam.; 19 1/2 by 5 in. diam.
Courtesy of William Traver Gallery

The Genies (Periwinkle Blue), 1996
Blown glass, 11 1/2 by 8 in. diam.; 18 by 7 in. diam.; 21 by 6 in. diam.
Courtesy of William Traver Gallery

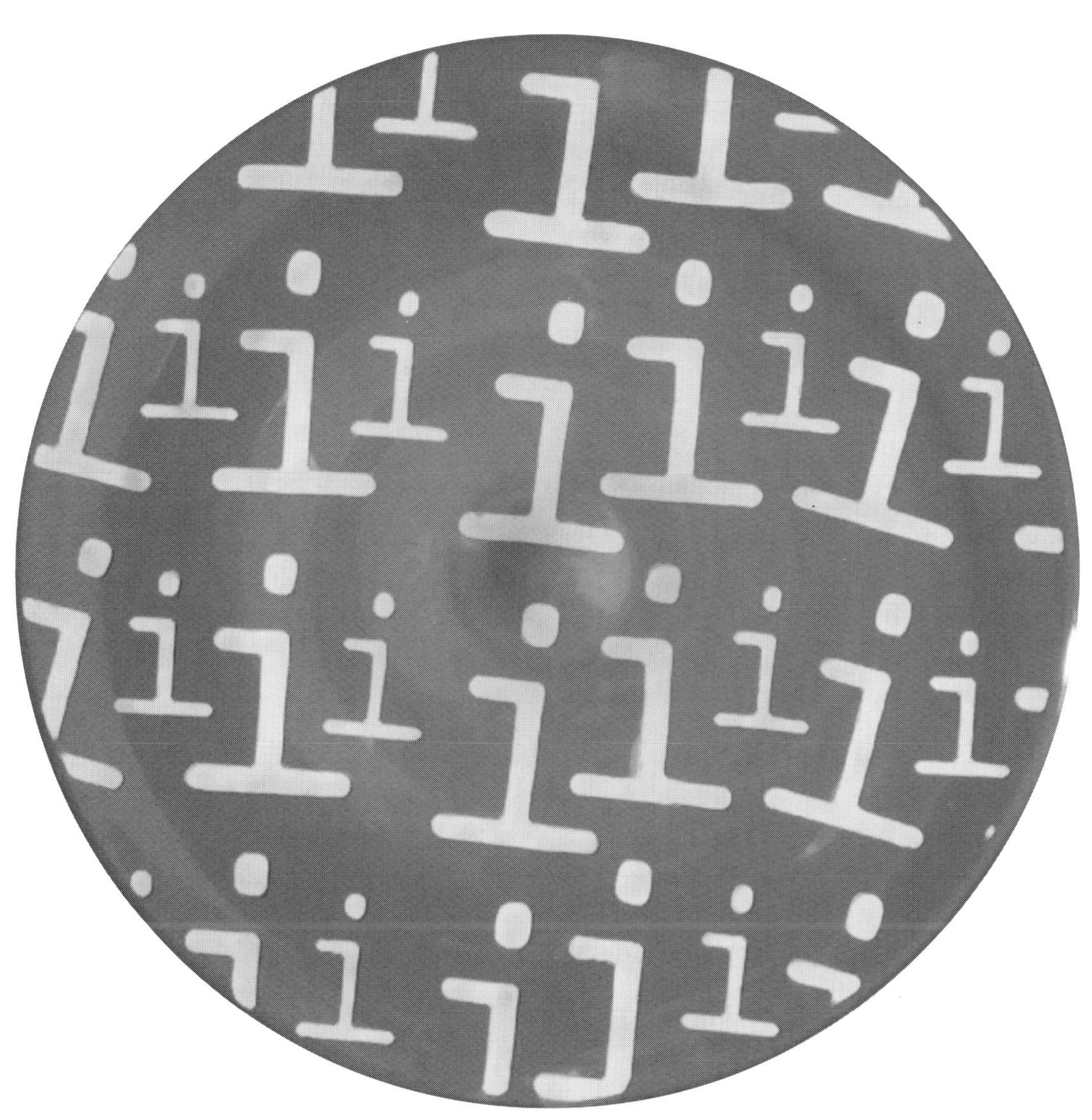

Asa Sandlund: **Courier**, 1996
Blown and sandblasted glass, 1 by 18 in. diam.
Courtesy of Vetri International Glass

Colophon

The text for this catalog has been set using New
Baskerville from Adobe Systems Incorporated. It
has been set in various sixes from 9pt. to 36pt.

The catalog has been printed on 100# gloss text
for the body and 10pt. Astralux C25 for the cover.

Perfect binding and film laminate for the cover
make up the catalog of 52 pages.